The First and Second Apologies ofJustin Martyr

Edited with Notes and Commentary by
Rev. Aaron Simms

The First and Second Apologies of Justin Martyr

Edited with Notes and Commentary by

Rev. Aaron Simms

ISBN: 0692745122
ISBN-13: 978-0692745120

Published by St. Polycarp Publishing House
www.stpolycarppublishinghouse.com
info@stpolycarppublishinghouse.com

Printed in the United States of America

DEDICATION

To my wife Amy and my children Molly and William, blessings from God.

CONTENTS

ACKNOWLEDGMENTS

Thank you to my wife Amy and my children Molly and William for all your love and support.

INTRODUCTION

Justin Martyr (also known as Justinus) was a mid-second century Christian writer. A Greek-speaking Gentile, he was born in Flavia Neapolis (present day Nablus) in Samaria and was martyred around 165 AD in Rome. He was familiar with Greek philosophy and shows an affinity for Socrates and Plato for reasons which he will explain in his Apologies.

He wrote his First and Second Apologies in approximately 150 AD. They are meant to be defenses (i.e. apologies in the classic sense of the term) of the Christian faith. It was likely that the two Apologies were actually one text, with the Second appended to the First. Justin addressed the First Apology to the Roman emperor Antoninus Pius and his sons Lucius and Verissimus (better known as Marcus Aurelius); the Second Apology was addressed to the Roman Senate. In both Apologies, Justin seeks to defend the Christian faith from the misrepresentations that were current in that day and to demonstrate that persecutions of Christians were unjust. Christians were loyal citizens, heirs of the best of philosophical tradition, and virtuous people. They ought therefore to be praised, rather than killed for their faith. Justin also prays that his readers will repent and turn to the truth which Christians proclaim. To assist with this goal, Justin expends much effort in describing what Christians believe and how they worship.

This present book reproduces both of Justin's Apologies, which were originally written in Greek. The English translation used here is the one provided by Alexander Roberts and James Donaldson (known as the Roberts-Donaldson English Translation) as part of the *Ante-Nicene Fathers* book series from the 19th century and is in the public domain. However, in a very few places I have selected more modern words than used in the original translation (given that the original translation is almost 200 years old). In addition, following each chapter of Justin's text, I have included notes and a brief commentary or summary in order to provide greater context to the thrust of Justin's argument and additional information where needed.

I have also included some tables as reference. These include a list of Roman emperors up to the fifth century, as well as a list of notable early Christian Church writers. One important note about the Roman emperors is that many times, particularly in the third and fourth centuries, there were co-emperors ruling somewhat concurrently, as well as usurpers to the throne. In addition, many times emperors ruled for less than a year before being murdered by a faction who wished to install their own emperor (particularly in 68/69 AD and 238 AD). Thus, there will be overlaps of the dates in the table.

My purpose in providing this edition of Justin's Apologies of the Christian Faith is to allow modern readers access to one of the great works of the early New Testament Church. Justin argues with a philosophical mind and provides early evidence of Christian belief and practice. I hope the reader enjoys this edition of Justin's *magnum opus*.

LIST OF ROMAN EMPERORS

Name	Dates of Reign	Important Events Related to the Church
Augustus	27 BC - 14 AD	Birth of Christ
Tiberius	14 AD - 37 AD	Crucifixion of Christ
Caligula	37 AD - 41 AD	
Claudius	41 AD - 54 AD	Expulsion of Jews from Rome on account of "Chrestus."
Nero	54 AD - 68 AD	Burning of Christians in Rome in 64 AD. Revolt of Judea/ Jerusalem in 66 AD (which will last until 70AD) - Vespasian (and later his son Titus) sent to put down the revolt.
Galba	68 AD - 69 AD	
Otho	69 AD	
Vitellius	69 AD	
Vespasian	69 AD - 79 AD	End of Jewish revolt in 70AD under Vespasian's son Titus, destruction of the Temple in Jerusalem.
Titus	79 AD - 81 AD	
Domitian	81 AD - 96 AD	Increased persecution of Christians. The Apostle John writes "Revelation" while exiled on the island of Patmos.

Name	Dates of Reign	Important Events Related to the Church
Nerva	96 AD - 98 AD	Bishop Clement of Rome writes "First Clement," a letter to the congregation in Corinth, referencing Paul's letters to them.
Trajan	98 AD - 117 AD	Letters between Trajan and Pliny the Younger, governor of Bithynia, are extant which discuss Christians.
Hadrian	117 AD - 138 AD	
Antoninus Pius	138 AD - 161 AD	Justin Martyr writes his "First Apology" addressed to Antoninus Pius and his adopted sons (and co-rulers) Marcus Aurelius and Lucius Verus. Justin Martyr writes his "Second Apology" addressed to the Roman Senate.
Marcus Aurelius	161 AD - 180 AD	
Lucius Verus	161 AD - 169 AD	
Commodus	177 AD - 192 AD	
Pertinax	193 AD	
Didius Julianus	193 AD	
Septimius Severus	193 AD - 211 AD	Tertullian writes his "Apology" during co-reign of Septimius Severus and Caracalla.
Caracalla	198 AD - 217 AD	
Geta	209 AD - 211 AD	
Macrinus and his son Diadumenian	217 AD - 218 AD	

Name	Dates of Reign	Important Events Related to the Church
Elagabalus	218 AD - 222 AD	
Severus Alexander	222 AD - 235 AD	
Maximinus I	235 AD - 238 AD	
Gordian I	238 AD	
Gordian II	238 AD	
Pupienus	238 AD	
Balbinus	238 AD	
Gordian III	238 AD - 244 AD	
Philip I	244 AD - 249 AD	
Philip II	247 AD - 249 AD	
Trajan Decius	249 AD - 251 AD	
Hostilian	251 AD	
Trebonianus Gallus	251 AD - 253 AD	
Aemilian	253 AD	
Valerian	253 AD - 260 AD	He issued edicts against Christians.
Gallienus	253 AD - 268 AD	In 260 AD, he issued edicts allowing toleration towards Christians.
Claudius Gothicus	268 AD - 270 AD	
Quintillus	270 AD	
Aurelian	270 AD - 275 AD	
Tacitus	275 AD - 276 AD	
Florian	276 AD	
Probus	276 AD - 282 AD	

Name	Dates of Reign	Important Events Related to the Church
Carus	282 AD - 283 AD	
Numerian	283 AD - 284 AD	
Carinus	283 AD - 285 AD	
Diocletian	284 AD - 305 AD	Major persecutor of the Church. Instituted intense Christian persecution in 303 AD with his co-rulers Maximian, Constantius I, and Galerius.
Maximian	286 AD - 305 AD	
Constantius I	305 AD - 306 AD (but "junior" co-emperor beginning in 293 AD)	
Galerius	305 AD - 311 AD (but "junior" co-emperor beginning in 293 AD)	
Severus II	306 AD - 307 AD	
Constantine the Great	306 AD - 337 AD	In 313 AD, he recognized religious freedom and right of Christians to worship freely. In 325 AD, he called the First Council of Nicaea to help unite the Church.
Maxentius	306 AD - 312 AD	
Maximinus II	311 AD - 313 AD	
Licinius I and Valerius Valens	308 AD - 324 AD	
Constantine II	337 AD - 340 AD	
Constantius II	337 AD - 361 AD	
Constans I	337 AD - 350 AD	

Name	Dates of Reign	Important Events Related to the Church
Vetranio	350 AD	
Julian	360 AD - 363 AD	Julian re-instituted intense persecutions of Christians.
Jovian	363 AD - 364 AD	
Valentinian I	364 AD - 375 AD	
Valens	364 AD - 378 AD	
Gratian	367 AD - 383 AD	
Valentinian II	375 AD - 392 AD	
Theodosius I	379 AD - 395 AD	
Arcadius	383 AD - 408 AD (Eastern Empire)	
Magnus Maximus and Flavius Victor	384 AD - 388 AD (Western Empire)	
Honorius	393 AD - 423 AD (Western Empire)	
Theodosius II	402 AD - 450 AD (Eastern Empire)	
Constantine III	407 AD - 411 AD (Western Empire)	Rome is sacked by the Visigoths in 410 AD - many Romans blamed Christians for the fall of Rome, which prompted St. Augustine to write "City of God."
Constantius III	421 AD (Western Empire)	
Joannes	423 AD - 425 AD (Western Empire)	
Valentinian III	424 AD - 455 AD (Western Empire)	St. Augustine publishes his work "City of God" in 426 AD
Marcian	450 AD - 457 AD (Eastern Empire)	

LIST OF NOTABLE EARLY CHRISTIAN WRITERS
AND WORKS

Name	Dates	Important Works
Clement of Rome	End of 1st Century AD	Epistle to Corinth
Anonymous	End of 1st Century AD	The Didache
Anonymous	2nd Century AD	Epistle of Barnabas
Anonymous	Early 2nd Century AD	Shepherd of Hermas
Ignatius of Antioch	Early 2nd Century AD	Epistles to Ephesus, Magnesia, Tralles, Rome, Philadelphia, and Smyrna Epistle to Polycarp
Polycarp of Smyrna	Early 2nd Century AD	Epistle to the Philippians
Anonymous	Mid 2nd Century AD	Epistle to Diognetus
Justin Martyr	Mid 2nd Century AD	First and Second Apologies
Irenaeus of Lyons	End of 2nd Century AD	Against Heresies Proof of the Apostolic Teaching
Athenagoras	End of 2nd Century AD	Embassy for the Christians
Tertullian	End of 2nd Century AD / Beginning of 3rd Century	Apology On the Spectacles A Demurrer to the Heretics' Plea (Many other works)
Clement of Alexandria	End of 2nd Century AD / Beginning of 3rd Century	An Invitation
Origin	End of 2nd Century AD / Beginning of 3rd Century	On First Principles Hexapla

Name	Dates	Important Works
Firmicus Maternus	Early 4th Century AD	Error of the Pagan Religions
St. Augustine	Mid 4th Century to Beginning of 5th AD	City of God Confessions (Many other works)

FIRST APOLOGY OF JUSTIN MARTYR

CHAPTER 1
Address

To the Emperor Titus Aelius Adrianus Antoninus Pius Augustus Caesar [1], and to his son Verissimus the Philosopher [2], and to Lucius the Philosopher, the natural son of Caesar, and the adopted son of Pius, a lover of learning [3], and to the sacred Senate, with the whole People of the Romans [4], I, Justin, the son of Priscus and grandson of Bacchius, natives of Flavia Neapolis in Palestine [5], present this address and petition in behalf of those of all nations who are unjustly hated and wantonly abused, myself being one of them.

Notes

[1] i.e. the emperor Antoninus Pius who ruled from 138 to 161 AD

[2] "Verissimus" was the nickname for Marcus Aurelius, meaning "most true," as a reference to his philosophical nature. He later succeeded Antoninus Pius as emperor and ruled jointly with Lucius until 169 AD.

[3] Lucius Verus, the adoptive brother of Marcus Aurelius. Lucius died in 169 AD, probably from smallpox. He was the natural son of Lucius Aelius Caesar. The emperor Hadrian had intended Lucius Aelius to succeed him; however, he died before he could take the throne. Lucius Verus became the adopted son of Antoninus Pius.

[4] The ancient, historic formulation of Rome was "Senatus Populusque Romanus," i.e. the Senate and People of Rome (abbreviated famously as SPQR).

[5] Flavia Neapolis is now known as Nablus and is located about 30 miles north of Jerusalem on the West Bank of the Jordan River. It was founded in 72 AD. Justin was a Greek-speaking Gentile.

Commentary

Justin addresses his letter to the current Roman emperor Antoninus Pius, his son Marcus Aurelius, and his adopted son Lucius Verus. Marcus Aurelius, in particular, was well-regarded as a Stoic philosopher and the collection of his thoughts has been published as his "Meditations." Justin's Apology is also addressed to the Senate and People of Rome (SPQR), which was the ancient formulation for the Roman state. Thus, his intended audience consists of the emperors, the Senate, and the people. Justin mentions his own native city and family of origin and notes that he is writing on behalf of those of all nations who are being unjustly treated, of whom he is one.

CHAPTER 2
Justice Demanded

Reason directs those who are truly pious and philosophical to honor and love only what is true, declining to follow traditional opinions, if these be worthless. For not only does sound reason direct us to refuse the guidance of those who did or taught anything wrong, but it is incumbent on the lover of truth [1], by all means, and if death be threatened, even before his own life, to choose to do and say what is right. Do you, then, since ye are called pious and philosophers [2], guardians of justice and lovers of learning, give good heed, and hearken to my address; and if ye are indeed such, it will be manifested.

For we have come, not to flatter you by this writing, nor please you by our address, but to beg that you pass judgment, after an accurate and searching investigation, not flattered by prejudice or by a desire of pleasing superstitious men, nor induced by irrational impulse or evil rumors which have long been prevalent, to give a decision which will prove to be against yourselves. For as for us, we reckon that no evil can be done us, unless we be convicted as evil-doers or be proved to be wicked men; and you, you can kill, but not hurt us.

Notes

[1] Justin is referring to the emperors' (i.e. Antoninus Pius, Marcus Aurelius and Lucius Verus) reputation for being philosophers.

[2] A play on words: "lover of truth" refers to the philosophers (i.e. "philo" = love, "sophia" = wisdom). "Pious" refers to Antoninus Pius.

Commentary

Justin appeals to the emperors' philosophical desires for the truth. He will make his argument based on the truth and not on flattery. The expectation is that since the emperors "love truth," they will listen to Justin and be convinced by his argument. Justin expects to prove that Christians profess the truth and are not criminals. Regardless, the worst that the emperors can do is kill them; they can not detach Christians from their hold on the truth or destroy their trust in Christ.

CHAPTER 3
Claim of Judicial Investigation

But lest any one think that this is an unreasonable and reckless utterance, we demand that the charges against the Christians be investigated, and that, if these be substantiated, they be punished as they deserve; [or rather, indeed, we ourselves will punish them.] [1] But if no one can convict us of anything, true reason forbids you, for the sake of a wicked rumor, to wrong blameless men, and indeed rather yourselves, who think fit to direct affairs, not by judgment, but by passion. And every sober-minded person will declare this to be the only fair and equitable adjustment, namely, that the subjects render an unexceptional account of their own life and doctrine; and that, on the other hand, the rulers should give their decision in obedience, not to violence and tyranny, but to piety and philosophy. For thus would both rulers and ruled reap benefit.

For even one of the ancients somewhere said, "Unless both rulers and ruled philosophize, it is impossible to make states blessed [2]." It is our task, therefore, to afford to all an opportunity of inspecting our life and teachings, lest, on account of those who are accustomed to be ignorant of our affairs, we should incur the penalty due to them for mental blindness [3]; and it is your business, when you hear us, to be found, as reason demands, good judges. For if, when ye have learned the truth, you do not what is just, you will be before God without excuse.

Notes

[1] The text in brackets is a possible scribal interpolation and may not be original to Justin's letter.

[2] From Plato's *Republic,* book 5.

[3] That is, if Christians do not explain their life and teachings, then they would be guilty of failing to illuminate those who do not know the faith.

Commentary

Justin appeals to his readers to actually investigate the charges against Christians to see if they are true. Christians, for their part (and Justin as their spokesman in this letter) will make their practices, beliefs, and teachings plainly known. The emperors, as the philosophers they are, should render sober judgment based on these facts, and not on the passions of the masses. If they do not, then they will have to render account before God.

CHAPTER 4
Christians Unjustly Condemned for Their Mere Name

By the mere application of a name, nothing is decided, either good or evil, apart from the actions implied in the name; and indeed, so far at least as one may judge from the name we are accused of, we are most excellent people [1]. But as we do not think it just to beg to be acquitted on account of the name, if we be convicted as evil-doers, so, on the other hand, if we be found to have committed no offense, either in the matter of thus naming ourselves, or of our conduct as citizens, it is your part very earnestly to guard against incurring just punishment, by unjustly punishing those who are not convicted. For from a name neither praise nor punishment could reasonably spring, unless something excellent or base in action be proved. And those among yourselves who are accused you do not punish before they are convicted; but in our case you receive the name as proof against us, and this although, so far as the name goes, you ought rather to punish our accusers. For we are accused of being Christians, and to hate what is excellent [2] is unjust. Again, if any of the accused deny the name, and say that he is not a Christian, you acquit him, as having no evidence against him as a wrong-doer; but if any one acknowledge that he is a Christian, you punish him on account of this acknowledgment.

Justice requires that you inquire into the life both of him who confesses and of him who denies, that by his deeds it may be apparent what kind of man each is. For as some who have been taught by the Master, Christ, not to deny Him, give encouragement to others when they are put to the question, so in all probability do those who lead wicked lives give occasion to those who, without consideration, take upon them to accuse all the Christians of impiety and wickedness. And this also is not right. For of philosophy, too, some assume the name and the garb who do nothing worthy of their profession; and you are well aware, that those of the ancients whose opinions and teachings were quite diverse, are yet all called by the one name of philosophers. And of these some taught atheism; and the poets who have flourished among you raise a laugh out of the uncleanness of Jupiter with his own children. And those who now adopt such instruction are not restrained by you; but, on the contrary, you bestow prizes and honors upon those who euphoniously insult the gods.

Notes

[1] Justin makes a play on words here and throughout this chapter. The Greek word *Christos* means Christ, while *chrestos* means good or excellent.

[2] i.e. *chrestian*

Commentary

Justin makes the point that Christians are condemned just based on the name alone, not due to any investigation into their actions. He uses the similarity of the words "Christos" and "chrestos" in this chapter to say that Christians are excellent and not worthy of condemnation. Yet, the lives of the accused should be looked into, because some who call themselves Christians are not true Christians and are therefore "not excellent." This is similar to the philosophers themselves, some of whom were no true philosophers and yet bore the name.

CHAPTER 5
Christians Charged with Atheism

Why, then, should this be? In our case, who pledge ourselves to do no wickedness, nor to hold these atheistic opinions, you do not examine the charges made against us; but, yielding to unreasoning passion, and to the instigation of evil demons, you punish us without consideration or judgment. For the truth shall be spoken; since of old these evil demons, effecting apparitions of themselves, both defiled women and corrupted boys, and showed such fearful sights to men, that those who did not use their reason in judging of the actions that were done, were struck with terror; and being carried away by fear, and not knowing that these were demons, they called them gods, and gave to each the name which each of the demons chose for himself [1].

And when Socrates endeavored, by true reason and examination, to bring these things to light, and deliver men from the demons, then the demons themselves, by means of men who rejoiced in iniquity, compassed his death, as an atheist and a profane person, on the charge that "he was introducing new divinities;" and in our case they display a similar activity [2]. For not only among the Greeks did reason (Logos) prevail to condemn these things through Socrates, but also among the Barbarians were they condemned by Reason (or the Word, the Logos) [3] Himself, who took shape, and became man, and was called Jesus Christ [4]; and in obedience to Him, we not only deny that they who did such things as these are gods, but assert that they are wicked and impious demons [5], whose actions will not bear comparison with those even of men desirous of virtue.

Notes

[1] The point being that the pagans worshipped demons who passed themselves off as gods.

[2] Socrates was convicted by the Athenians of impiety (because he did not worship the gods) and forced to drink hemlock.

[3] The Greek word *logos* can mean reason or word, and some of the Greek philosophers used it in the sense of the creative, ordering force in the world. Christians identified the Logos with Jesus Christ; i.e. He is the Word/Logos of God made flesh, the one through whom all things were created and through whom all things are being restored (see Genesis 1 for the Father speaking forth the Word/Logos to create and John 1 for the Word/Logos made flesh).

[4] Note the connection with the introduction of John's Gospel as well as the creative acts of the Word (Logos) in Genesis 1.

[5] The Greeks used the word *daimon* to mean a god, but Christians made the point that these were evil spirits.

Commentary

Justin makes the point that the pagans worshipped gods who were actually evil demons. These demons pretend to be gods and lash out at those who know the truth. The Greek philosopher Socrates was put to death at the behest of these demons, and they lash out now against Christians. Some of the Greek philosophers (Plato in particular) believed that the logos (reason, word) was the creative and ordering force in the world who came from God. They got very close to the truth. Justin states that this logos became man as Jesus Christ; in this he is closely following the introduction to John's Gospel. This is also a critical connection point with the Roman emperors, who were philosophers themselves. They would have been familiar with the Greek concept of the logos, and so Justin's point is important that this logos is Jesus Christ.

CHAPTER 6
Charge of Atheism Refuted

Hence are we called atheists [1]. And we confess that we are atheists, so far as gods of this sort are concerned, but not with respect to the most true God, the Father of righteousness and temperance and the other virtues, who is free from all impurity. But both Him, and the Son (who came forth from Him and taught us these things, and the host of the other good angels who follow and are made like to Him), and the prophetic Spirit, we worship and adore, knowing them in reason and truth, and declaring without grudging to every one who wishes to learn, as we have been taught [2].

Notes

[1] i.e. because they do not worship the demons

[2] Christians worship the Triune God only: Father, Son, and Holy Spirit.

Commentary

The point here is that Christians are not atheists. It is true that they do not worship the "gods" of the Romans, which are simply demons; in that Christians are "atheists." However, Christians worship the true God who is Father, Son, and Holy Spirit. This is not a secret wisdom or religion; Christians will declare this God to everyone who desires to learn about Him. In fact, this is the point of Justin's letter; i.e. to declare the true God to the Roman emperors, Senate, and people.

CHAPTER 7
Each Christian Must Be Tried By His Own Life

But some one will say, "Some have ere now been arrested and convicted as evil-doers." For you condemn many, many a time, after inquiring into the life of each of the accused severally, but not on account of those of whom we have been speaking [1]. And this we acknowledge, that as among the Greeks those who teach such theories as please themselves are all called by the one name "Philosopher," though their doctrines be diverse, so also among the Barbarians this name on which accusations are accumulated is the common property of those who are and those who seem wise. For all are called Christians [2]. Wherefore we demand that the deeds of all those who are accused to you be judged, in order that each one who is convicted may be punished as an evil-doer, and not as a Christian; and if it is clear that any one is blameless, that he may be acquitted, since by the mere fact of his being a Christian he does no wrong. For we will not require that you punish our accusers; they being sufficiently punished by their present wickedness and ignorance of what is right.

Notes

[1] That is, there are some Christians who have been convicted of crimes. This is just, if they have actually committed a crime, and not convicted falsely at the instigation of the demons (i.e. "of those of whom we have been speaking").

[2] i.e. there are some "Christians" who use the name, but who are not true Christians

Commentary

Justin again makes the appeal that Christians be judged based on their deeds, and not on the name "Christian" alone. Christians were usually condemned just for the mere fact of being Christian, even though they had done nothing to deserve the condemnation of the law. The pagan rejoinder which Justin anticipates is, "Yes, but some Christians have been convicted of real crimes." Justin acknowledges that this is true, but points out that not all who call themselves "Christians" are real Christians, just as not all who call themselves "Philosopher" are real philosophers. Therefore, Christians ought to be judged for their deeds and not on account of the name only, just as others are judged before the law.

CHAPTER 8
Christians Confessed Their Faith in God

And reckon ye that it is for your sakes we have been saying these things; for it is in our power, when we are examined, to deny that we are Christians; but we would not live by telling a lie [1]. For, impelled by the desire of the eternal and pure life, we seek the abode that is with God, the Father and Creator of all, and hasten to confess our faith, persuaded and convinced as we are that they who have proved to God by their works that they followed Him, and loved to abide with Him where there is no sin to cause disturbance, can obtain these things. This, then, to speak shortly, is what we expect and have learned from Christ, and teach.

And Plato, in like manner, used to say that Rhadamanthus and Minos [2] would punish the wicked who came before them; and we say that the same thing will be done, but at the hand of Christ, and upon the wicked in the same bodies united again to their spirits which are now to undergo everlasting punishment; and not only, as Plato said, for a period of a thousand years [3]. And if any one say that this is incredible or impossible, this error of ours is one which concerns ourselves only, and no other person, so long as you cannot convict us of doing any harm.

Notes

[1] That is, Christians bear witness to the truth, even to death; they do so in the hopes of converting their persecutors through this witness.

[2] Minos and Rhadamanthus were considered by the Greeks/Romans to be judges of the underworld.

[3] Justin refers here to the resurrection of the body and eternity.

Commentary

Justin states that Christians are witnesses to the truth even to their deaths. They would rather die than live a lie or betray their Savior. In so doing, they hope that their persecutors will be converted through their bold witness. In addition, they expect the resurrection of the body and the judgment of Christ. Those who are evil will go to everlasting punishment. If the Romans think all this is ridiculous, then the only harm done is to Christians for holding these beliefs. What harm does one person's belief do to another? Why must the Romans kill Christians?

CHAPTER 9
Folly of Idol Worship

And neither do we honor with many sacrifices and garlands of flowers such deities as men have formed and set in shrines and called gods; since we see that these are soulless and dead, and have not the form of God (for we do not consider that God has such a form as some say that they imitate to His honor), but have the names and forms of those wicked demons which have appeared [1]. For why need we tell you who already know, into what forms the craftsmen, carving and cutting, casting and hammering, fashion the materials [2]? And often out of vessels of dishonor, by merely changing the form, and making an image of the requisite shape, they make what they call a god; which we consider not only senseless, but to be even insulting to God, who, having ineffable glory and form, thus gets His name attached to things that are corruptible, and require constant service [3].

And that the artificers of these are both intemperate, and, not to enter into particulars, are practiced in every vice, you very well know; even their own girls who work along with them they corrupt [4]. What infatuation! that dissolute men should be said to fashion and make gods for your worship, and that you should appoint such men the guardians of the temples where they are enshrined; not recognizing that it is unlawful even to think or say that men are the guardians of gods.

Notes

[1] Justin again references the fact that the pagan "gods" are demons.

[2] i.e. men make the "gods" out of various materials and art

[3] i.e. the true God has no form

[4] i.e. the artisans corrupt young girls

Commentary

Justin makes the point that the Romans make their "gods" out of materials. How strange is it that gods require the service of men to not only make them, but also tend them? In addition, the craftsmen themselves are immoral, corrupting their female helpers and engaging in various evils. The true God does not require sinful men to make Him, nor tend Him. He has no form, but rather gives form to men.

CHAPTER 10
How God is to be Served

But we have received by tradition that God does not need the material offerings which men can give, seeing, indeed, that He Himself is the provider of all things. And we have been taught, and are convinced, and do believe, that He accepts those only who imitate the excellences which reside in Him, temperance, and justice, and philanthropy, and as many virtues as are peculiar to a God who is called by no proper name [1].

And we have been taught that He in the beginning did of His goodness, for man's sake, create all things out of unformed matter; and if men by their works show themselves worthy of this His design, they are deemed worthy, and so we have received--of reigning in company with Him, being delivered from corruption and suffering. For as in the beginning He created us when we were not, so do we consider that, in like manner, those who choose what is pleasing to Him are, on account of their choice, deemed worthy of incorruption and of fellowship with Him [2]. For the coming into being at first was not in our own power; and in order that we may follow those things which please Him, choosing them by means of the rational faculties He has Himself endowed us with, He both persuades us and leads us to faith [3].

And we think it for the advantage of all men that they are not restrained from learning these things, but are even urged thereto. For the restraint which human laws could not effect, the Word, inasmuch as He is divine, would have effected, had not the wicked demons, taking as their ally the lust of wickedness which is in every man, and which draws variously to all manner of vice, scattered many false and profane accusations, none of which attach to us [4].

Notes

[1] In contrast to the pagan gods who were named, many after men and women.

[2] Justin speaks here of God's creation of all things and of the resurrection of the body. In this, he is echoing the first and third articles of the later Apostles' Creed.

[3] An important point; i.e. God created us and brings us to faith, it is not in our own power to do either.

[4] i.e. the demon "gods" spread slanders against Christians

Commentary

God has no name. For this reason, the Hebrews called Him simply "Yahweh," meaning essentially "He who is and causes to be." God Himself gave His name as simply "I Am" (see Exodus 3:13ff). He created everything in the beginning and will raise up all bodies at the resurrection. Just as people did not do anything to create themselves, so too do they not create faith themselves; God does both. He and His people (Christians) want all people to know the truth about Him. In an effort to combat this, the demons spread false rumors about Christians.

CHAPTER 11
What Kingdom Christians Look For

And when you hear that we look for a kingdom, you suppose, without making any inquiry, that we speak of a human kingdom; whereas we speak of that which is with God [1], as appears also from the confession of their faith made by those who are charged with being Christians, though they know that death is the punishment awarded to him who so confesses. For if we looked for a human kingdom, we should also deny our Christ, that we might not be slain; and we should strive to escape detection, that we might obtain what we expect. But since our thoughts are not fixed on the present, we are not concerned when men cut us off; since also death is a debt which must at all events be paid [2].

Notes

[1] See, for example, John 18:36 and Rev. 1:6.

[2] i.e. death comes to all, it is only a matter of when

Commentary

The kingdom of God is not a human kingdom or a place. It is the reign of God into which Christians have been brought. Christians hold to God's kingdom, even to death, knowing that death must come anyway at some point. Thus, Christians confess their faith up to the end, trusting in God.

CHAPTER 12
Christians Live as Under God's Eye

And more than all other men are we your helpers and allies in promoting peace, seeing that we hold this view, that it is alike impossible for the wicked, the covetous, the conspirator, and for the virtuous, to escape the notice of God, and that each man goes to everlasting punishment or salvation according to the value of his actions. For if all men knew this, no one would choose wickedness even for a little, knowing that he goes to the everlasting punishment of fire; but would by all means restrain himself, and adorn himself with virtue, that he might obtain the good gifts of God, and escape the punishments. For those who, on account of the laws and punishments you impose, endeavor to escape detection when they offend (and they offend, too, under the impression that it is quite possible to escape your detection, since you are but men), those persons, if they learned and were convinced that nothing, whether actually done or only intended, can escape the knowledge of God, would by all means live decently on account of the penalties threatened, as even you yourselves will admit [1].

But you seem to fear lest all men become righteous, and you no longer have any to punish. Such would be the concern of public executioners, but not of good princes. But, as we before said, we are persuaded that these things are prompted by evil spirits, who demand sacrifices and service even from those who live unreasonably; but as for you, we presume that you who aim at [a reputation for] piety and philosophy will do nothing unreasonable. But if you also, like the foolish, prefer custom to truth, do what you have power to do. But just so much power have rulers who esteem opinion more than truth, as robbers have in a desert [2]. And that you will not succeed is declared by the Word, than whom, after God who begat Him, we know there is no ruler more kingly and just. For as all shrink from succeeding to the poverty or sufferings or obscurity of their fathers, so whatever the Word forbids us to choose, the sensible man will not choose.

That all these things should come to pass, I say, our Teacher foretold, He who is both Son and Apostle [3] of God the Father of all and the Ruler, Jesus Christ; from whom also we have the name of Christians. Whence we become more assured of all the things He taught us, since whatever He beforehand foretold should come to pass, is seen in fact coming to pass; and this is the work of God, to tell of a thing before it happens, and as it was foretold so to show it happening.

It were possible to pause here and add no more, reckoning that we demand what is just and true; but because we are well aware that it is not easy suddenly to change a mind possessed by ignorance, we intend to add a few things, for the sake of persuading those who love the truth, knowing that it is not impossible to put ignorance to flight by presenting the truth.

Notes

[1] The argument is that Christians make the best citizens because they know that God sees their thoughts and actions.

[2] That is, the rulers who govern at the whim of the people soon find that they have no real power, but are rather at the mercy of those whom they are meant to rule.

[3] Apostle means "he who is sent with the authority of the one who sent him." Justin's point here is that Christ is the Apostle of the Father; i.e. the Father sent him with His authority. Then, Christ sent his Apostles with his authority.

Commentary

Justin's argument is that Christians are good citizens because they know that they are constantly being seen by God. They do not need to be compelled by law to do good, they do good for the sake of God. They are not like those people who disobey the law when convenient or when they believe they are at low risk of being caught. Instead, Christians are always driven to do good.

Justin expects the emperors to be persuaded that the persecution of Christians is unjust. Yet, these events were foretold by Christ. In this, Justin probably has in mind Jesus' words in the Gospels which foretell the persecution of Christians as well as the tribulations foretold in Revelation. He also points out that Christ is the Son of God and vested with his Father's authority. Justin says that what he has previously written ought to be enough to convince sound rulers of the injustice of Christian persecution, but that he will continue with his argument in order to convince them of the truth.

CHAPTER 13
Christians Serve God Rationally

What sober-minded man, then, will not acknowledge that we are not atheists, worshipping as we do the Maker of this universe, and declaring, as we have been taught, that He has no need of streams of blood and libations and incense; whom we praise to the utmost of our power by the exercise of prayer and thanksgiving for all things wherewith we are supplied, as we have been taught that the only honor that is worthy of Him is not to consume by fire what He has brought into being for our sustenance, but to use it for ourselves and those who need, and with gratitude to Him to offer thanks by invocations and hymns for our creation, and for all the means of health, and for the various qualities of the different kinds of things, and for the changes of the seasons; and to present before Him petitions for our existing again in incorruption through faith in Him [1].

Our teacher of these things is Jesus Christ, who also was born for this purpose, and was crucified under Pontius Pilate, procurator of Judaea, in the times of Tiberius Caesar [2]; and that we reasonably worship Him, having learned that He is the Son of the true God Himself, and holding Him in the second place, and the prophetic Spirit in the third, we will prove [3]. For they proclaim our madness to consist in this, that we give to a crucified man a place second to the unchangeable and eternal God, the Creator of all; for they do not discern the mystery that is herein, to which, as we make it plain to you, we pray you to give heed.

Notes

[1] Note the parallels with the First Article of the Apostles' Creed.

[2] Tiberius Caesar was emperor of Rome from 14 AD to 37 AD. Pontius Pilate was the fifth prefect of Judaea from 26 AD to 36 AD. Jesus was crucified in either 30 AD or 33 AD, most likely the later date. Note that Justin calls Pilate a "procurator," which was a non-military official, whereas a "prefect" was a military officer with both civil and military authority. By Justin's time the Roman territories which were previously governed by prefects were now governed by procurators, so Justin is using the then-current terminology.

[3] Note the parallels with the Second and Third Articles of the Apostles' Creed.

Commentary

Here Justin again makes the case that Christians are not "atheists" as the Romans suppose. Rather, Christians worship the God who created everything. He is the Maker who has given us the creation for us to enjoy and put to good use. Then, Justin discusses the Son, Jesus Christ, and provides details on when he was crucified; these details would have been sufficient for the Romans to know to what time period Justin is referring. Finally, Justin mentions the Holy Spirit. These sections where Justin talks about the Father, Son, and Holy Spirit parallel the three Articles of the Apostles' Creed. Justin is confessing Christian belief in a Triune God, or Trinity, before the Romans. This is a mystery, as Justin notes, but he will attempt to explain it better to his readers.

CHAPTER 14
The Demons Misrepresent Christian Doctrine

For we forewarn you to be on your guard, lest those demons whom we have been accusing should deceive you, and quite divert you from reading and understanding what we say. For they strive to hold you their slaves and servants; and sometimes by appearances in dreams, and sometimes by magical impositions, they subdue all who make no strong opposing effort for their own salvation.

And thus do we also, since our persuasion by the Word, stand aloof from them (i.e., the demons), and follow the only unbegotten God through His Son — we who formerly delighted in fornication, but now embrace chastity alone; we who formerly used magical arts, dedicate ourselves to the good and unbegotten God; we who valued above all things the acquisition of wealth and possessions, now bring what we have into a common stock, and communicate to every one in need; we who hated and destroyed one another, and on account of their different manners would not live with men of a different tribe, now, since the coming of Christ, live familiarly with them, and pray for our enemies, and endeavor to persuade those who hate us unjustly to live conformably to the good precepts of Christ, to the end that they may become partakers with us of the same joyful hope of a reward from God the ruler of all.

But lest we should seem to be reasoning sophistically [1], we consider it right, before giving you the promised explanation, to cite a few precepts given by Christ Himself. And be it yours, as powerful rulers, to inquire whether we have been taught and do teach these things truly. Brief and concise utterances fell from Him, for He was no sophist, but His word was the power of God.

Notes

[1] That is, Christians are not sophists; i.e. those who make their point with clever, but frequently false, arguments.

Commentary

It is the demons, again Justin says, who want to keep people from believing in Christ. They hold people captive and do not want to let them go. Yet, the Word of God converts people to faith and makes them new. Justin contrasts how the lives of Christians were before conversion in comparison to how they are after they have been brought to faith in Christ. He says that he will next cite some words which come from Christ himself. Christ is no sophist, who tries to convince people based on clever rhetoric, but rather he speaks with the authority of God.

CHAPTER 15
What Christ Himself Taught

Concerning chastity, He [1] uttered such sentiments as these: "Whosoever looketh upon a woman to lust after her, hath committed adultery with her already in his heart before God." And, "If thy right eye offend thee, cut it out; for it is better for thee to enter into the kingdom of heaven with one eye, than, having two eyes, to be cast into everlasting fire." And, "Whosoever shall marry her that is divorced from another husband, committeth adultery [2]." And, "There are some who have been made eunuchs of men, and some who were born eunuchs, and some who have made themselves eunuchs for the kingdom of heaven's sake; but all cannot receive this saying [3]." So that all who, by human law, are twice married, are in the eye of our Master sinners, and those who look upon a woman to lust after her. For not only he who in act commits adultery is rejected by Him, but also he who desires to commit adultery: since not only our works, but also our thoughts, are open before God. And many, both men and women, who have been Christ's disciples from childhood, remain pure at the age of sixty or seventy years; and I boast that I could produce such from every race of men.

For what shall I say, too, of the countless multitude of those who have reformed intemperate habits, and learned these things? For Christ called not the just nor the chaste to repentance, but the ungodly, and the licentious, and the unjust; His words being, "I came not to call the righteous, but sinners to repentance [4]." For the heavenly Father desires rather the repentance than the punishment of the sinner.

And of our love to all, He taught thus: "If ye love them that love you, what new thing do ye? for even fornicators do this. But I say unto you, Pray for your enemies, and love them that hate you, and bless them that curse you, and pray for them that despitefully use you [5]".

And that we should communicate to the needy, and do nothing for glory, He said, "Give to him that asketh, and from him that would borrow turn not away; for if ye lend to them of whom ye hope to receive, what new thing do ye? even the publicans do this. Lay not up for yourselves treasure upon earth, where moth and rust doth corrupt, and where robbers break through; but lay up for yourselves treasure in heaven, where neither moth nor rust doth corrupt. For what is a man profited, if he shall gain the whole world, and lose his own soul? or what shall a man give in exchange for it? Lay up treasure, therefore, in heaven, where neither moth nor rust doth corrupt [6]."

And, "Be ye kind and merciful, as your Father also is kind and merciful, and maketh His sun to rise on sinners, and the righteous, and the wicked. Take no thought what ye shall eat, or what ye shall put on: are ye not better than the birds and the beasts? And God feedeth them. Take no thought, therefore, what ye shall eat, or what ye shall put on; for your heavenly Father knoweth that ye have need of these things. But seek ye the kingdom of heaven, and all these things shall be added unto you. For where his treasure is, there also is the mind of a man [7]." And, "Do not these things to be seen of men; otherwise ye have no reward from your Father which is in heaven [8]."

Notes

[1] i.e. Jesus Christ

[2] cf. Matthew 5:28-29, 32

[3] cf. Matthew 19:12

[4] cf. Matthew 9:13

[5] cf. Matthew 5:44, 46; Luke 6:28

[6] cf. Luke 6:30, 34; Matthew 6:19-20, 16:26

[7] cf. Luke 6:36; Matthew 5:45, 6:21, 26-26,33

[8] cf. Matthew 6:1

Commentary

Justin cites some of the sayings of Jesus to show that Christians are enjoined by their God to live righteous lives. He focuses first on sexual purity and Christ's emphasis on either marriage or chaste living as God-pleasing. Yet, God is gracious and merciful and forgives sin. This is why Christ came, to call sinners to himself to bestow upon them his forgiveness so that they may be reconciled to God. Similarly, Christians themselves are called to do good to those who have wronged them. They are also encouraged to forsake the desire for wealth and pursue instead the kingdom of God, trusting that God will provide all things which are needed.

CHAPTER 16
Concerning Patience and Swearing

And concerning our being patient of injuries, and ready to serve all, and free from anger, this is what He said: "To him that smiteth thee on the one cheek, offer also the other; and him that taketh away thy cloak or coat, forbid not. And whosoever shall be angry, is in danger of the fire. And every one that compelleth thee to go with him a mile, follow him two. And let your good works shine before men, that they, seeing them, may glorify your Father which is in heaven [1]." For we ought not to strive; neither has He desired us to be imitators of wicked men, but He has exhorted us to lead all men, by patience and gentleness, from shame and the love of evil. And this indeed is proved in the case of many who once were of your way of thinking, but have changed their violent and tyrannical disposition, being overcome either by the constancy which they have witnessed in their neighbors' lives [2], or by the extraordinary forbearance they have observed in their fellow-travelers when defrauded, or by the honesty of those with whom they have transacted business.

And with regard to our not swearing at all, and always speaking the truth, He enjoined as follows: "Swear not at all; but let your yea be yea, and your nay, nay; for whatsoever is more than these cometh of evil [3]." And that we ought to worship God alone, He thus persuaded us: "The greatest commandment is, Thou shalt worship the Lord thy God, and Him only shalt thou serve, with all thy heart, and with all thy strength, the Lord God that made thee [4]." And when a certain man came to Him and said, "Good Master," He answered and said, "There is none good but God only, who made all things [5]."

And let those who are not found living as He taught, be understood to be no Christians, even though they profess with the lip the precepts of Christ; for not those who make profession, but those who do the works, shall be saved, according to His word: "Not every one who saith to Me, Lord, Lord, shall enter into the kingdom of heaven, but he that doeth the will of My Father which is in heaven. For whosoever heareth Me, and doeth My sayings, heareth Him that sent Me. And many will say unto Me, Lord, Lord, have we not eaten and drunk in Thy name, and done wonders? And then will I say unto them, Depart from Me, ye workers of iniquity. Then shall there be wailing and gnashing of teeth, when the righteous shall shine as the sun, and the wicked are sent into everlasting fire. For many shall come in My name, clothed outwardly in sheep's clothing, but inwardly being ravening wolves. By their works ye shall know them. And every tree that bringeth not forth good fruit, is hewn down and cast into the fire [6]." And as to those who are not living pursuant to these His teachings, and are

Christians only in name, we demand that all such be punished by you.

Notes

[1] cf. Luke 6:29; Matthew 6:16, 22, 41

[2] i.e. Christian neighbors. The point is that the way Christians live is a witness to their faith.

[3] cf. Matthew 5:27,34

[4] cf. Mark 12:30

[5] cf. Matthew 19:16-17

[6] cf. Matthew 7:15-16,19ff, 13:42; Luke 13:26

Commentary

Justin again quotes from Jesus's words which relate to bearing with one another, having patience, not swearing, and living righteously. Earlier, Justin had made the point to the emperors that Christians ought not to be judged based simply on the name "Christian," but rather on their actions. Here, he makes a similar point that God Himself knows who really is a Christian and who simply appropriates the name falsely. True Christians are known by their works. Therefore, Justin urges the emperors to punish those who call themselves "Christian," but who are not living as Christians and are therefore not true Christians. This again re-emphasizes Justin's point that the emperors ought to judge Christians not on the basis of the name, but rather on the basis of their works.

CHAPTER 17
Christ Taught Civil Obedience

And everywhere we, more readily than all men, endeavor to pay to those appointed by you the taxes both ordinary and extraordinary [1], as we have been taught by Him; for at that time some came to Him and asked Him, if one ought to pay tribute to Caesar; and He answered, "Tell Me, whose image does the coin bear?" And they said, "Caesar's." And again He answered them, "Render therefore to Caesar the things that are Caesar's, and to God the things that are God's [2]."

Whence to God alone we render worship, but in other things we gladly serve you, acknowledging you as kings and rulers of men, and praying that with your kingly power you be found to possess also sound judgment. But if you pay no regard to our prayers and frank explanations, we shall suffer no loss, since we believe (or rather, indeed, are persuaded) that every man will suffer punishment in eternal fire according to the merit of his deed, and will render account according to the power he has received from God, as Christ intimated when He said, "To whom God has given more, of him shall more be required [3]."

Notes

[1] i.e. both annual taxes and any special assessments

[2] cf. Matthew 12:17ff

[3] cf. Luke 12:48

Commentary

Justin emphasizes that Christians have a duty to obey civil government in the realm of authority given it by God. God Himself rules over all things and has instituted civil authority for the benefit of humanity. Thus, Christians pay taxes, pray for the rulers, and give whatever obedience is right to those in civil authority. Yet, they will not worship government or its rulers. Instead, they worship God only, as is right. Justin prays that the emperors will know and acknowledge this, because they - as rulers - have a heavy burden of responsibility for which they will have to account before God at the judgment.

CHAPTER 18
Proof of Immortality and the Resurrection

For reflect upon the end of each of the preceding kings, how they died the death common to all, which, if it issued in insensibility, would be a godsend to all the wicked. But since sensation remains to all who have ever lived, and eternal punishment is laid up (i.e., for the wicked), see that ye neglect not to be convinced, and to hold as your belief, that these things are true [1].

For let even necromancy, and the divinations you practice by immaculate children [2], and the evoking of departed human souls, and those who are called among the magi [3], Dream-senders and Assistant-spirits (Familiars), and all that is done by those who are skilled in such matters — let these persuade you that even after death souls are in a state of sensation; and those who are seized and cast about by the spirits of the dead, whom all call demoniacs or madmen [4]; and what you repute as oracles, both of Amphilochus, Dodona, Pytho [5], and as many other such as exist; and the opinions of your authors, Empedocles [6] and Pythagoras [7], Plato [8] and Socrates [9], and the pit of Homer [10], and the descent of Ulysses to inspect these things, and all that has been uttered of a like kind.

Such favor as you grant to these, grant also to us, who not less but more firmly than they believe in God; since we expect to receive again our own bodies, though they be dead and cast into the earth, for we maintain that with God nothing is impossible.

Notes

[1] That is to say, "You ought to believe that the Christian faith is true, since you will face death and judgment one day."

[2] Justin refers to the pagan practice of sacrificing infants (even those not born yet) to inspect their entrails for fortunes.

[3] Magi is used here to refer to spirits who either inspire dreams ("Dream-senders") or watch over people ("Assistant-spirits" or "Familiars").

[4] i.e. the possessed

[5] Amphilochus was believed in Greek mythology to have founded many oracles; Dodona was in Epirus and the oldest Greek oracle; Pytho was another name for the famous oracle at Delphi.

[6] Empedocles was a Greek philosopher of the 5th century BC. He believed in reincarnation.

[7] Pythagoras was a Greek philosopher of the 6th century BC. He believed in some form of reincarnation or transmigration of the soul.

[8] Plato was a Greek philosopher of the 5th century BC. He believed in the immortality of the soul.

[9] Socrates was a Greek philosopher of the 5th Century BC. He believed in a form of immortality of the soul.

[10] In the *Odyssey* (Book XI, line 25), Homer describes Ulysses as using his sword to dig a trench in order to gather up the souls of the dead around him.

Commentary

Justin addresses the topic of the soul and eternity. He points out that people ought to be concerned about the truth, because it has eternal import on the future of the soul. For support, he references various Greek philosophers who also taught about the soul's existence after bodily death. However, Christians do not only believe that the soul exists after death, but also that the body will be resurrected. This may seem impossible to man, since the body dies and decays, but God can do this because nothing is impossible to Him.

CHAPTER 19
The Resurrection Possible

And to any thoughtful person would anything appear more incredible, than, if we were not in the body, and some one were to say that it was possible that from a small drop of human seed bones and sinews and flesh be formed into a shape such as we see? For let this now be said hypothetically: if you yourselves were not such as you now are, and born of such parents [and causes], and one were to show you human seed and a picture of a man, and were to say with confidence that from such a substance such a being could be produced, would you believe before you saw the actual production? No one will dare to deny [that such a statement would surpass belief].

In the same way, then, you are now incredulous because you have never seen a dead man rise again. But as at first you would not have believed it possible that such persons could be produced from the small drop, and yet now you see them thus produced, so also judge ye that it is not impossible that the bodies of men, after they have been dissolved, and like seeds resolved into earth, should in God's appointed time rise again and put on incorruption. For what power worthy of God those imagine who say, that each thing returns to that from which it was produced, and that beyond this not even God Himself can do anything, we are unable to conceive; but this we see clearly, that they would not have believed it possible that they could have become such and produced from such materials, as they now see both themselves and the whole world to be.

And that it is better to believe even what is impossible to our own nature and to men, than to be unbelieving like the rest of the world, we have learned; for we know that our Master Jesus Christ said, that "what is impossible with men is possible with God [1]," and, "Fear not them that kill you, and after that can do no more; but fear Him who after death is able to cast both soul and body into hell [2]." And hell is a place where those are to be punished who have lived wickedly, and who do not believe that those things which God has taught us by Christ will come to pass.

Notes

[1] cf. Matthew 19:26

[2] cf. Matthew 10:28

Commentary

Justin uses the analogy of birth to illustrate how the resurrection of the body is possible. He points out that if one were to look at the "seed" of a man and then a picture of a man, you would never believe that the one would become the other, except for having seen it yourself. Similarly, it may be impossible to believe that God will bring life to dead and decayed bodies (like seeds), but He will bring it to pass. We believe that humans come from seemingly nothing; we ought to believe that God will bring us back to life again from seemingly nothing.

CHAPTER 20
Heathen Analogies to Christian Doctrine

And the Sibyl and Hystaspes [1] said that there should be a dissolution by God of things corruptible. And the philosophers called Stoics [2] teach that even God Himself shall be resolved into fire, and they say that the world is to be formed anew by this revolution; but we understand that God, the Creator of all things, is superior to the things that are to be changed. If, therefore, on some points we teach the same things as the poets and philosophers whom you honor, and on other points are fuller and more divine in our teaching, and if we alone afford proof of what we assert, why are we unjustly hated more than all others?

For while we say that all things have been produced and arranged into a world by God, we shall seem to utter the doctrine of Plato; and while we say that there will be a burning up of all, we shall seem to utter the doctrine of the Stoics: and while we affirm that the souls of the wicked, being endowed with sensation even after death, are punished, and that those of the good being delivered from punishment spend a blessed existence, we shall seem to say the same things as the poets and philosophers; and while we maintain that men ought not to worship the works of their hands, we say the very things which have been said by the comic poet Menander [3], and other similar writers, for they have declared that the workman is greater than the work.

Notes

[1] i.e. pagan oracles

[2] The emperor Marcus Aurelius, one of the intended readers of Justin's letter, was a Stoic philosopher.

[3] Menander was a Greek comedic playwright of the late 4th century BC.

Commentary

Justin illuminates various points of contact between Christian belief and the teachings of the philosophers. His main point is that if Christian doctrine is similar to various philosophical teachings, then why are Christians persecuted? This argument should have special resonance for someone like Marcus Aurelius, a philosopher himself. It is interesting to note that many Christians in the first few centuries found kindred spirits, of sorts, in some of the Greek philosophers (particularly Plato). They believed that God had revealed some truth to the philosophers which anticipated the coming of Christ to reveal the full truth. This is why Justin is not shy about pointing out correspondences between philosophy and Christian belief; all truth comes from God. Certainly, the pagan philosophers missed the mark in many ways, since they did not have the full revelation of Christ. Thus, Justin writes his letter to make this full revelation to his readers in an effort to bring them to the truth.

CHAPTER 21
Analogies to the History of Christ

And when we say also that the Word, who is the first-birth [1] of God, was produced without sexual union, and that He, Jesus Christ, our Teacher, was crucified and died, and rose again, and ascended into heaven, we propound nothing different from what you believe regarding those whom you esteem sons of Jupiter [2]. For you know how many sons your esteemed writers ascribed to Jupiter [3]: Mercury, the interpreting word and teacher of all; Aesculapius, who, though he was a great physician, was struck by a thunderbolt, and so ascended to heaven; and Bacchus too, after he had been torn limb from limb; and Hercules, when he had committed himself to the flames to escape his toils; and the sons of Leda, and Dioscuri; and Perseus, son of Danae; and Bellerophon, who, though sprung from mortals, rose to heaven on the horse Pegasus. For what shall I say of Ariadne, and those who, like her, have been declared to be set among the stars? And what of the emperors who die among yourselves, whom you deem worthy of deification, and in whose behalf you produce some one who swears he has seen the burning Caesar rise to heaven from the funeral pyre?

And what kind of deeds are recorded of each of these reputed sons of Jupiter [4], it is needless to tell to those who already know. This only shall be said, that they are written for the advantage and encouragement of youthful scholars; for all reckon it an honorable thing to imitate the gods [5]. But far be such a thought concerning the gods from every well-conditioned soul, as to believe that Jupiter himself, the governor and creator of all things, was both a parricide and the son of a parricide, and that being overcome by the love of base and shameful pleasures, he came in to Ganymede and those many women whom he had violated and that his sons did like actions. But, as we said above, wicked devils perpetrated these things. And we have learned that those only are deified who have lived near to God in holiness and virtue [6]; and we believe that those who live wickedly and do not repent are punished in everlasting fire.

Notes

[1] i.e. the first born

[2] Justin means to show that Christian belief is not all that foreign to the Romans.

[3] The Greeks and Romans tended to make men and women into gods as offspring of Jupiter/Zeus. Justin goes on to name various people, including

emperors, who were later deified as sons or daughters of Jupiter.

[4] The "sons of Jupiter" refers to the Roman gods.

[5] Justin writes this with a sense of sarcasm or irony, as the Roman and Greek gods were known for their immoral behavior, as he will go on to demonstrate.

[6] Justin uses the word "deified" here in the sense of immortal bliss; the point he is making is that Christians are "deified" by receiving everlasting life with God, while pagans are punished in everlasting fire.

Commentary

Justin here demonstrates that the Christian belief that Jesus Christ was born of a virgin, was crucified, died, and rose again to life is not that odd of a belief. The aim is to acclimate his readers to Christian belief. The pagan myths have similar stories, although in incomplete and corrupted form. Many of the Greek and Roman "gods" were simply men and women who were later deified by admirers and then considered to be sons and daughters of Jupiter. Yet, Jupiter is a false god and was believed to have perpetuated many immoral acts. Christians believe, on the other hand, that only those who live true lives with the true God will receive eternal life with Him.

CHAPTER 22
Analogies to the Sonship of Christ

Moreover, the Son of God called Jesus, even if only a man by ordinary generation, yet, on account of His wisdom, is worthy to be called the Son of God; for all writers call God the Father of men and gods. And if we assert that the Word of God was born of God in a peculiar manner, different from ordinary generation, let this, as said above, be no extraordinary thing to you, who say that Mercury is the angelic word of God [1]. But if any one objects that He was crucified, in this also He is on a par with those reputed sons of Jupiter of yours, who suffered as we have now enumerated. For their sufferings at death are recorded to have been not all alike, but diverse; so that not even by the peculiarity of His sufferings does He seem to be inferior to them; but, on the contrary, as we promised in the preceding part of this discourse, we will now prove Him superior — or rather have already proved Him to be so — for the superior is revealed by His actions. And if we even affirm that He was born of a virgin, accept this in common with what you accept of Perseus [2]. And in that we say that He made whole the lame, the paralytic, and those born blind, we seem to say what is very similar to the deeds said to have been done by Aesculapius [3].

Notes

[1] Mercury was believed to be the messenger (i.e. angel) of God by the Romans.

[2] In Greek mythology, Perseus was believed to be the son of Zeus and Danaë.

[3] Aesculapius was the Greek god of medicine.

Commentary

Justin again seeks to demonstrate that what Christians say about Jesus should not sound so strange to the Romans. In this, he is seeking to connect with his Roman readers to help them better understand Christian faith and its truth, as opposed to the Greek and Roman myths. His point is not that Christians "copied" the Greeks and Romans; rather, his point is that the Romans thought the Christian beliefs absurd, and yet they believed somewhat similar things about their gods.

CHAPTER 23
The Argument

And that this [1] may now become evident to you — (firstly) that whatever we assert in conformity with what has been taught us by Christ, and by the prophets who preceded Him, are alone true, and are older than all the writers who have existed; that we claim to be acknowledged, not because we say the same things as these writers said, but because we say true things: and (secondly) that Jesus Christ is the only proper Son who has been begotten by God, being His Word and first-begotten, and power; and, becoming man according to His will, He taught us these things for the conversion and restoration of the human race: and (thirdly) that before He became a man among men, some, influenced by the demons before mentioned, related beforehand, through the instrumentality of the poets, those circumstances as having really happened, which, having fictitiously devised, they narrated, in the same manner as they have caused to be fabricated the scandalous reports against us of infamous and impious actions, of which there is neither witness nor proof--we shall bring forward the following proof.

Notes

[1] i.e. the superiority of Jesus over the pagan gods

Commentary

Justin proposes to make a three-fold argument proving the superiority of Jesus over the gods of the Romans. First, he will show that only the Christian faith is true and that it is older than everything else, particularly the writers of the Greek and Roman myths; chapters 24 through 29 will address this topic. Second, he will demonstrate that Jesus is both the only-begotten Son of God as well as true man; chapters 30 through 53 will address this topic. Third, he will show that the demons inspired the Greek and Roman poets to create myths which have some correspondence to the life of Jesus in order to sow confusion and discord; Justin touched on this topic in the previous chapters, but chapters 54 and following will address this further. Thus, Justin is now coming to the meat of his letter.

CHAPTER 24
Varieties of Heathen Worship

In the first place [we furnish proof], because, though we say things similar to what the Greeks say, we only are hated on account of the name of Christ, and though we do no wrong, are put to death as sinners; other men in other places worshipping trees and rivers, and mice and cats and crocodiles, and many irrational animals [1]. Nor are the same animals esteemed by all; but in one place one is worshipped, and another in another, so that all are profane in the judgment of one another, on account of their not worshipping the same objects. And this is the sole accusation you bring against us, that we do not reverence the same gods as you do, nor offer to the dead libations and the savor of fat, and crowns for their statues, and sacrifices. For you very well know that the same animals are with some esteemed gods, with others wild beasts, and with others sacrificial victims [2].

Notes

[1] Justin references various pagan practices, particularly those of the Egyptians.

[2] That is, some animals are worshiped by people, while also being considered just wild animals by others, and then also being sacrificed by others as victims to their "gods."

Commentary

Justin again points out that Christians are hated for the sake of the name of Christ. Many people have various religious practices, and yet the Roman authorities punish Christians alone for their faith.

CHAPTER 25
False Gods Abandoned by Christians

And, secondly, because we — who, out of every race of men, used to worship Bacchus the son of Semele, and Apollo the son of Latona (who in their loves with men did such things as it is shameful even to mention), and Proserpine and Venus (who were maddened with love of Adonis [1], and whose mysteries also you celebrate), or Aesculapius, or some one or other of those who are called gods — have now, through Jesus Christ, learned to despise these, though we be threatened with death for it, and have dedicated ourselves to the unbegotten and impossible God; of whom we are persuaded that never was he goaded by lust of Antiope, or such other women, or of Ganymede [2], nor was rescued by that hundred-handed giant whose aid was obtained through Thetis [3], nor was anxious on this account that her son Achilles should destroy many of the Greeks because of his concubine Briseis [4]. Those who believe these things we pity, and those who invented them we know to be devils.

Notes

[1] Adonis was a cultic figured worshiped in various mystery religions.

[2] In Greek mythology, Zeus raped the woman Antiope, among other women; he also kidnapped the boy Ganymede.

[3] Thetis was a sea nymph in Greek mythology. She rescued Zeus by calling the hundred-handed monster Aegaeon (also called Briareus).

[4] Achilles was the son of Thetis, and Briseis was the woman whom he won in battle as his prize.

Commentary

Justin makes a distinction between the true God whom Christians worship and the false gods of the pagans. First, he calls attention to men and women - such as Bacchus, Apollo, Proserpine, Venus, and Aesculapius - who were later worshiped as gods, with various myths attached to them. Then, he calls attention to the shameful things the god Zeus was believed to have done. Unlike these "gods," the Christian God is not just a man, nor is He a capricious, sinful god such as Zeus. Rather, He is both true God and true, perfect man, known to Christians as Jesus Christ.

CHAPTER 26
Magicians Not Trusted by Christians

And, thirdly, because after Christ's ascension into heaven the devils put forward certain men who said that they themselves were gods; and they were not only not persecuted by you, but even deemed worthy of honors. T

There was a Samaritan, Simon [1], a native of the village called Gitto, who in the reign of Claudius Caesar, and in your royal city of Rome, did mighty acts of magic, by virtue of the art of the devils operating in him. He was considered a god, and as a god was honored by you with a statue, which statue was erected on the river Tiber, between the two bridges, and bore this inscription, in the language of Rome: — "Simoni Deo Sancto," "To Simon the holy God." And almost all the Samaritans, and a few even of other nations, worship him, and acknowledge him as the first god; and a woman, Helena, who went about with him at that time, and had formerly been a prostitute, they say is the first idea generated by him.

And a man, Menander [2], also a Samaritan, of the town Capparetaea, a disciple of Simon, and inspired by devils, we know to have deceived many while he was in Antioch by his magical art. He persuaded those who adhered to him that they should never die, and even now there are some living who hold this opinion of his.

And there is Marcion [3], a man of Pontus, who is even at this day alive, and teaching his disciples to believe in some other god greater than the Creator. And he, by the aid of the devils, has caused many of every nation to speak blasphemies, and to deny that God is the maker of this universe, and to assert that some other being, greater than He, has done greater works.

All who take their opinions from these men, are, as we before said, called Christians; just as also those who do not agree with the philosophers in their doctrines, have yet in common with them the name of philosophers given to them. And whether they perpetrate those fabulous and shameful deeds [4] —the upsetting of the lamp, and promiscuous intercourse, and eating human flesh — we know not; but we do know that they are neither persecuted nor put to death by you, at least on account of their opinions.

But I have a treatise against all the heresies that have existed already composed, which, if you wish to read it, I will give you [5].

Notes

[1] i.e. Simon Magus. He is referenced also in Acts 8:9-24. He was a 1st century AD Gnostic and magician who tried to buy influence and power in the Church.

[2] Menander succeeded Simon and was also a Gnostic and magician of the 1st century AD.

[3] Marcion was a Gnostic of the late 1st and 2nd centuries AD. He rejected the Old Testament and proposed the existence of a greater god than He who is revealed in the Old Testament. He died in 160 AD, thus helping to date Justin's *Apology*.

[4] Justin refers to the false charges which the Romans laid against Christians. The "upsetting of the lamp" refers to orgies (i.e. the lamps were turned over by dogs to put out the lights before the participants engaged in the activities).

[5] Justin also wrote *Against Marcion* and a *Refutation of All Heresies*, which are both, unfortunately, lost.

Commentary

Justin here mentions a few of the more prominent heretics of the early Church. Simon Magus, Menander, and Marcion all did and taught things contrary to the Truth. Simon and Menander also claimed to be magicians. These men are called "Christians," but not rightly; this is similar to how not all those who are called "philosophers" are actually true philosophers. The Church has therefore rejected these men and their teachings, because they are not true Christians. The main point which Justin wants to make here is that the Romans oddly do not persecute the followers of these heresies; they just persecute the true Christians. The implication is that the Romans everywhere let false belief flourish, only seeking to extinguish the confession of the Truth.

CHAPTER 27
Guilt of Exposing Children

But as for us, we have been taught that to expose newly-born children is the part of wicked men; and this we have been taught lest we should do any one an injury, and lest we should sin against God, first, because we see that almost all so exposed (not only the girls, but also the males) are brought up to prostitution [1]. And as the ancients are said to have reared herds of oxen, or goats, or sheep, or grazing horses, so now we see you rear children only for this shameful use; and for this pollution a multitude of females and hermaphrodites, and those who commit unmentionable iniquities, are found in every nation. And you receive the hire of these, and duty and taxes from them, whom you ought to exterminate from your realm. And any one who uses such persons, besides the godless and infamous and impure intercourse, may possibly be having intercourse with his own child, or relative, or brother. And there are some who prostitute even their own children and wives, and some are openly mutilated for the purpose of sodomy; and they refer these mysteries to the mother of the gods, and along with each of those whom you esteem gods there is painted a serpent, a great symbol and mystery. Indeed, the things which you do openly and with applause, as if the divine light were overturned and extinguished [2], these you lay to our charge; which, in truth, does no harm to us who shrink from doing any such things, but only to those who do them and bear false witness against us.

Notes

[1] The Romans would "expose" unwanted children on the road, allowing anyone to take them, or allowing them to die. Justin's point is that these children were often taken by those who ran prostitution houses in order to raise the children as prostitutes.

[2] Justin's remark is a reference to the Roman charge that Christians "overturned and extinguished" the lamps at their feasts so that they could engage in debauchery.

Commentary

The Romans tended to place unwanted children on the roads, exposing them to either death or to the whims of those who picked them up. Justin makes the point that Christians regard the disposal of children, as if they were trash, as the work of "wicked men." These children are often brought up as prostitutes and the Romans use them and celebrate prostitution as if it were God-pleasing. Strangely, the Romans accuse Christians of doing these sorts of things, even though they approve of them. Justin points out, though, that Christians do no such things.

CHAPTER 28
God's care for men

For among us the prince of the wicked spirits is called the serpent, and Satan, and the devil, as you can learn by looking into our writings [1]. And that he would be sent into the fire with his host, and the men who follow him, and would be punished for an endless duration, Christ foretold.

For the reason why God has delayed to do this, is His regard for the human race. For He foreknows some about to be saved by repentance, and some not yet perhaps born [2]. In the beginning He made the human race with the power of thought and of choosing the truth and doing right, so that all men are without excuse before God; for they have been born rational and contemplative.

And if any one disbelieves that God cares for these things [3], he will thereby either insinuate that God does not exist, or he will assert that though He exists He delights in vice, or exists like a stone, and that neither virtue nor vice are anything, but only in the opinion of men these things are reckoned good or evil. And this is the greatest profanity and wickedness.

Notes

[1] i.e. the Scriptures

[2] The present author has adopted the alternative literal reading here for this sentence, as it makes more sense in the context. The original translation read: "For He foreknows that some are to be saved by repentance, some even that are perhaps not yet born."

[3] That is, "these things" meaning man's salvation.

Commentary

In the previous chapter, Justin made the point that the Romans often used the image of the serpent in connection with their gods, who condoned wicked practices. Here he states that Christians call Satan the serpent. The reason the Romans do wicked things is because they are actually worshipping demons over whom Satan rules as their prince. At the end of the age, though, God will throw Satan, his demons, and all who follow them into hell for eternity. This judgment is delayed, however, for the sake of those who will repent and believe in Jesus Christ. The God the

Christians worship is a God who cares about people and who desires all to be saved; He is the one from whom all good comes.

CHAPTER 29
Continence of Christians

And again [we fear to expose children], lest some of them be not picked up, but die, and we become murderers. But whether we marry, it is only that we may bring up children; or whether we decline marriage, we live continently.

And that you may understand that promiscuous intercourse is not one of our mysteries [1], one of our number a short time ago presented to Felix the governor in Alexandria a petition, craving that permission might be given to a surgeon to make him an eunuch. For the surgeons there said that they were forbidden to do this without the permission of the governor. And when Felix absolutely refused to sign such a permission, the youth remained single, and was satisfied with his own approving conscience, and the approval of those who thought as he did. And it is not out of place, we think, to mention here Antinous, who was alive but lately, and whom all were prompt, through fear, to worship as a god, though they knew both who he was and what his origin [2].

Notes

[1] "Mysteries" in the sense of religious or worship practices.

[2] Antinous was the male lover of the Roman emperor Hadrian. He was deified after his death in 130 AD.

Commentary

Justin contrasts Christian sexual mores with that of the Romans. First, he points out that Christians have two proper states, either that of marriage or that of chastity. What is more, the purpose of marriage is to "bring up children," in contradiction to the Roman practice of exposing their children on the roads when unwanted. For those unmarried, they do not engage in fornication. Justin uses the example of a man in Alexandria, Egypt who wanted to be made a eunuch, and when denied the surgery still lived a chaste life. He juxtaposes this with the example of the emperor Hadrian who took a lover.

CHAPTER 30
Was Christ not a magician?

But lest any one should meet us with the question [1], What should prevent that He whom we call Christ, being a man born of men, performed what we call His mighty works by magical art, and by this appeared to be the Son of God? we will now offer proof, not trusting mere assertions, but being of necessity persuaded by those who prophesied [of Him] before these things came to pass, for with our own eyes we behold things that have happened and are happening just as they were predicted; and this will, we think appear even to you the strongest and truest evidence.

Notes

[1] Justin poses a rhetorical question.

Commentary

Justin anticipates the objection by the Romans that perhaps Christ just appeared to be the Son of God because he was a very good magician. He states that he will demonstrate that Christ was foretold in the past and that he fulfilled the prophecies which pointed to him. To do this, Justin will draw on the Old Testament in the following chapters.

CHAPTER 31
Of the Hebrew prophets

There were, then, among the Jews certain men who were prophets of God, through whom the prophetic Spirit published beforehand things that were to come to pass, ere ever they happened. And their prophecies, as they were spoken and when they were uttered, the kings who happened to be reigning among the Jews at the several times carefully preserved in their possession, when they had been arranged in books by the prophets themselves in their own Hebrew language [1]. And when Ptolemy king of Egypt formed a library, and endeavored to collect the writings of all men, he heard also of these prophets, and sent to Herod, who was at that time king of the Jews, requesting that the books of the prophets be sent to him [2]. And Herod the king did indeed send them, written, as they were, in the foresaid Hebrew language. And when their contents were found to be unintelligible to the Egyptians, he again sent and requested that men be commissioned to translate them into the Greek language. And when this was done, the books remained with the Egyptians, where they are until now.

They are also in the possession of all Jews throughout the world; but they, though they read, do not understand what is said, but count us foes and enemies; and, like yourselves, they kill and punish us whenever they have the power, as you can well believe. For in the Jewish war which lately raged, Barchochebas, the leader of the revolt of the Jews, gave orders that Christians alone should be led to cruel punishments, unless they would deny Jesus Christ and utter blasphemy [3].

In these books, then, of the prophets we found Jesus our Christ foretold as coming, born of a virgin, growing up to man's estate, and healing every disease and every sickness, and raising the dead, and being hated, and unrecognized, and crucified, and dying, and rising again, and ascending into heaven, and being, and being called, the Son of God. We find it also predicted that certain persons should be sent by Him into every nation to publish these things, and that rather among the Gentiles [than among the Jews] men should believe on Him [4]. And He was predicted before He appeared, first 5000 years before, and again 3000, then 2000, then 1000, and yet again 800; for in the succession of generations prophets after prophets arose [5].

Notes

[1] i.e. the Hebrew Scriptures, known to Christians as the Old Testament

[2] Ptolemy Philadelphus was the king of Egypt in the mid-third century BC. He supported the Library of Alexandria and had the Hebrew Scriptures (i.e. the Old Testament) translated into Greek, which is what Justin is referring to here in this section. This Greek translation became known as the Septuagint and was the standard version of the Scriptures in use during Jesus' era. That is to say, when Jesus and others in the New Testament quote from the Old Testament, they are most often quoting from the Greek Septuagint. However, it was actually Eleazer the high priest, and not Herod, to whom Ptolemy requested the books; this may be Justin's error or that of a later copyist.

[3] Justin is referring to the Jewish Bar Kokhba revolt from 132 to 136 AD. After the war, the Romans deported the Jews from Judea, merged the territory with Syria, and renamed Jerusalem "Aelia Capitolina," barring Jews from the land.

[4] Justin summarizes the Christian interpretation of various Old Testament prophecies concerning the Christ. The scope of these are outside this present work, but the reader is humbly directed to consider *The Christian Story… as seen through the Old Testament* by the present author which treats this topic in more detail.

[5] These dates are interesting. Justin's "5,000 years" reference probably refers to God's first promise of the Christ, given in Genesis 3:15 (called the *Protevangelium*); this would mean Justin viewed the creation of the world as occurring around 5000 BC. The flood of Noah was around 3000 BC; Abraham was around 2000 BC; David was around 1000 BC; Isaiah was around 800 BC. Justin rounds to the nearest century, but his dates generally correspond to orthodox, conservative Christian views of the Old Testament timeline.

Commentary

Justin makes the point that Jesus Christ was foretold long ago in the Hebrew Scriptures. These writings were translated into Greek and disseminated throughout the land before Christ came. In them, the prophets foretold who Christ would be and what he would do. Thus, Jesus is known to be the true Christ because he fulfilled these prophecies. Justin also gives some dates which correspond to Old Testament chronology and which serve to attest to the ancient nature of the Christian faith.

CHAPTER 32
Christ predicted by Moses

Moses then, who was the first of the prophets, spoke in these very words: "The scepter shall not depart from Judah, nor a lawgiver from between his feet, until He come for whom it is reserved; and He shall be the desire of the nations, binding His foal to the vine, washing His robe in the blood of the grape [1]." It is yours to make accurate inquiry, and ascertain up to whose time the Jews had a lawgiver and king of their own [2]. Up to the time of Jesus Christ, who taught us, and interpreted the prophecies which were not yet understood, [they had a lawgiver] as was foretold by the holy and divine Spirit of prophecy through Moses, "that a ruler would not fail the Jews until He should come for whom the kingdom was reserved" (for Judah was the forefather of the Jews, from whom also they have their name of Jews); and after He (i.e., Christ) appeared, you began to rule the Jews, and gained possession of all their territory.

And the prophecy, "He shall be the expectation of the nations," signified that there would be some of all nations who should look for Him to come again. And this indeed you can see for yourselves, and be convinced of by fact. For of all races of men there are some who look for Him who was crucified in Judea, and after whose crucifixion the land was straightway surrendered to you as spoil of war [3].

And the prophecy, "binding His foal to the vine, and washing His robe in the blood of the grape," was a significant symbol of the things that were to happen to Christ, and of what He was to do. For the foal of an ass stood bound to a vine at the entrance of a village, and He ordered His acquaintances to bring it to Him then; and when it was brought, He mounted and sat upon it, and entered Jerusalem, where was the vast temple of the Jews which was afterwards destroyed by you [4].

And after this He was crucified, that the rest of the prophecy might be fulfilled. For this "washing His robe in the blood of the grape" was predictive of the passion He was to endure, cleansing by His blood those who believe on Him. For what is called by the Divine Spirit through the prophet "His robe," are those men who believe in Him in whom abideth the seed of God, the Word. And what is spoken of as "the blood of the grape," signifies that He who should appear would have blood, though not of the seed of man, but of the power of God.

And the first power after God the Father and Lord of all is the Word, who is also the Son; and of Him we will, in what follows, relate how He took flesh and became man. For as man did not make the blood of the vine, but

God, so it was hereby intimated that the blood should not be of human seed, but of divine power, as we have said above.

And Isaiah, another prophet, foretelling the same things in other words, spoke thus: "A star shall rise out of Jacob, and a flower shall spring from the root of Jesse; and His arm shall the nations trust [5]." And a star of light has arisen, and a flower has sprung from the root of Jesse — this Christ. For by the power of God He was conceived by a virgin of the seed of Jacob, who was the father of Judah, who, as we have shown, was the father of the Jews; and Jesse was His forefather according to the oracle, and He was the son of Jacob and Judah according to lineal descent.

Notes

[1] cf. Genesis 49:10-11

[2] Herod the Great was the last king of the Jews, dying in 4 BC. In 6 AD, the Romans took direct control over Judea.

[3] Justin is probably referring to the Roman victory over Judea in 70 AD following the Jewish revolt in 66 AD.

[4] cf. Mark 11:1ff; Matthew 21:1ff; Luke 19:28ff

[5] cf. Isaiah 11:1

Commentary

Justin covers a lot of ground in this chapter. First, he quotes from Jacob's dying blessing to his son Judah in Genesis 49 to demonstrate how it is a prophecy which points to Christ. The message of the prophecy is that the Christ would come once the people of Judah lost their king. This was fulfilled during the time of Herod the Great. He was the last king of Judah, during whose reign Jesus was born (probably 6/5 BC), and died in 4 BC. The point is that Jesus Christ came at the time which was foretold. In addition, he is Christ for all nations, not just the Jews; this is demonstrated by the fact that people throughout the Roman empire worship Christ. Finally, the prophecy from Genesis shows that Christ would die and cleanse humanity through his blood of sacrifice. Justin closes by promising to speak more of Christ's incarnation and birth from a virgin.

CHAPTER 33
Manner of Christ's birth predicted

And hear again how Isaiah in express words foretold that He should be born of a virgin; for he spoke thus: "Behold, a virgin shall conceive, and bring forth a son, and they shall say for His name, God with us [1]." For things which were incredible and seemed impossible with men, these God predicted by the Spirit of prophecy as about to come to pass, in order that, when they came to pass, there might be no unbelief, but faith, because of their prediction.

But lest some, not understanding the prophecy now cited, should charge us with the very things we have been laying to the charge of the poets who say that Jupiter went in to women through lust, let us try to explain the words. This, then, "Behold, a virgin shall conceive," signifies that a virgin should conceive without intercourse [2]. For if she had had intercourse with any one whatever, she was no longer a virgin; but the power of God having come upon the virgin, overshadowed her, and caused her while yet a virgin to conceive. And the angel of God who was sent to the same virgin at that time brought her good news, saying, "Behold, thou shalt conceive of the Holy Ghost, and shalt bear a Son, and He shall be called the Son of the Highest, and thou shalt call His name Jesus; for He shall save His people from their sins, [3]" — as they who have recorded all that concerns our Savior Jesus Christ have taught, whom we believed, since by Isaiah also, whom we have now adduced, the Spirit of prophecy declared that He should be born as we intimated before.

It is wrong, therefore, to understand the Spirit and the power of God as anything else than the Word, who is also the first-born of God, as the foresaid prophet Moses declared; and it was this which, when it came upon the virgin and overshadowed her, caused her to conceive, not by intercourse, but by power. And the name Jesus in the Hebrew language means Soter (Savior) in the Greek tongue [4]. Wherefore, too, the angel said to the virgin, "Thou shalt call His name Jesus, for He shall save His people from their sins [5]." And that the prophets are inspired [6] by no other than the Divine Word, even you, as I fancy, will grant.

Notes

[1] cf. Isaiah 7:14. Also note that the word Emmanuel is in the actual verse and means "God with us;" Justin quotes the meaning of the name for his readers.

[2] Justin makes it clear that Jesus' mother was a virgin in the normal understanding of the word.

[3] cf. Luke 1:32, Mathew 1:21

[4] The Hebrew form of Jesus is Joshua. Both mean "Yahweh saves" or "Yahweh is salvation."

[5] cf. Matthew 1:21, 23

[6] Justin uses the greek word *theophorountai* here, which is translated "inspired." The original word connotes those who are completely under the influence of a god. The Romans would have considered the oracles to be so; Justin makes the point here that the prophets were under the complete influence of the Word of the one true God.

Commentary

Justin addresses the topic of the virgin birth of Jesus Christ. The prophets foretold this manner of his birth, particularly Isaiah. In addition, he was born to a true virgin who conceived by the power of the Holy Spirit. This was not like the pagan myths regarding Jupiter. Rather, it was the true God coming into the world through the virgin birth. The one who was born was Jesus the Christ. His name means salvation, for that is what he came to bring to humanity. All this was in fulfillment of the prophecies given in the Hebrew Scriptures (i.e. the Old Testament).

CHAPTER 34
Place of Christ's birth foretold

And hear what part of earth He was to be born in, as another prophet, Micah, foretold. He spoke thus: "And thou, Bethlehem, the land of Judah, art not the least among the princes of Judah; for out of thee shall come forth a Governor, who shall feed My people [1]." Now there is a village in the land of the Jews, thirty-five stadia [2] from Jerusalem, in which Jesus Christ was born, as you can ascertain also from the registers of the taxing made under Cyrenius, your first procurator in Judea [3].

Notes

[1] cf. Micah 5:2

[2] The stadium was a Greek and Roman unit of distance, equal to approximately 185 meters.

[3] Justin refers to Luke's account in the Gospel, cf. Luke 2:2ff. Judea was considered to be linked to the Roman imperial province of Syria, which was governed by a "legate" or governor of the praetorian rank. In contrast, Judea was governed, beginning in 6 AD, by a prefect of the lower equestrian rank (Pontius Pilate was the fifth prefect of Judea). There has always been an issue with interpreting Luke's account, because Quirinius (also spelled Cyrenius) is known to be the legate of Syria from 6 AD to 12 AD, but Jesus was born prior to the death of Herod the Great in 4 BC; thus, making the dates appear incompatible. However, the Roman governor who ruled Syria from 4 BC to 1 BC is not known for certain. Justin probably calls Quirinius the "first procurator in Judea" because Judea was placed under direct Roman control, and under the general supervision of Quirinius, in 6 AD.

Commentary

Justin quotes the prophet Micah to show that the birthplace of Jesus in Bethlehem was also foretold in the Old Testament. He refers his readers to the taxation registers made during the time, if they wanted to verify that Jesus was born there. However, as mentioned above in note 3, there has always been an issue with the dates of Quirinius' governorship of Syria, the death of Herod the Great, and the birth of Jesus.

Jesus was born prior to Herod's death in 4 BC, but Quirinius did not enter office until 6 AD. Thus, Luke's statement can not be taken as commonly translated: "This was the first registration when Quirinius was governor of Syria." Instead, another way to read the Greek is: "This was the registration before Quirinius was governor of Syria." This is a valid reading of the Greek which has the advantage of agreeing with the known dates regarding Herod and Quirinius, as well as using the census begun by Quirinius in 6 AD as a reference point. This is important because the census of 6 AD, and the direct Roman takeover of Judea at that time, caused a revolt which was well-known to the Jews and Romans. Thus, Luke may be using this event as his reference point to state that the census of Jesus' time was "before" the more well-known census of 6 AD during which the province revolted.

CHAPTER 35
Other prophecies fulfilled

And how Christ after He was born was to escape the notice of other men until He grew to man's estate, which also came to pass, hear what was foretold regarding this. There are the following predictions: "Unto us a child is born, and unto us a young man is given, and the government shall be upon His shoulders [1];" which is significant of the power of the cross, for to it, when He was crucified, He applied His shoulders, as shall be more clearly made out in the ensuing discourse. And again the same prophet Isaiah, being inspired by the prophetic Spirit, said, "I have spread out my hands to a disobedient and gainsaying people, to those who walk in a way that is not good. They now ask of me judgment, and dare to draw near to God [2]."

And again in other words, through another prophet, He says, "They pierced My hands and My feet, and for My vesture they cast lots [3]." And indeed David, the king and prophet, who uttered these things, suffered none of them; but Jesus Christ stretched forth His hands, being crucified by the Jews speaking against Him, and denying that He was the Christ. And as the prophet spoke, they tormented Him, and set Him on the judgment-seat, and said, Judge us. And the expression, "They pierced my hands and my feet," was used in reference to the nails of the cross which were fixed in His hands and feet. And after He was crucified they cast lots upon His vesture, and they that crucified Him parted it among them. And that these things did happen, you can ascertain from the Acts of Pontius Pilate [4].

And we will cite the prophetic utterances of another prophet, Zephaniah [5], to the effect that He was foretold expressly as to sit upon the foal of an ass and to enter Jerusalem. The words are these: "Rejoice greatly, O daughter of Zion; shout, O daughter of Jerusalem: behold, thy King cometh unto thee; lowly, and riding upon an ass, and upon a colt the foal of an ass [6].

Notes

[1] cf. Isaiah 9:6

[2] cf. Isaiah 65:2; Isaiah 58:2

[3] cf. Psalm 22:16

[4] Justin refers to a collection of reports regularly made by Pontius Pilate

to the emperor Tiberius as part of his official duties. This book, if it existed, has been lost to history, although an apocryphal account exists within the fourth century "Gospel of Nicodemus."

[5] Actually Zechariah, probably a slip up on Justin's part or of a later copyist.

[6] cf. Zechariah 9:9.

Commentary

Justin again cites various Old Testament prophecies concerning Christ, this time with a view to showing that he came appearing as a humble man. He was crucified, dying a criminal's death on the cross. He entered into Jerusalem on a donkey (as opposed to the Roman practice of parading conquering generals and emperors into town on a chariot). Justin also quotes from Psalm 22, which is significant because Jesus cries out the opening words of this Psalm while on the cross: "My God, my God, why have you forsaken me?" (Matthew 27:46; Mark 15:34). The Psalm itself speaks in the person of the suffering Christ, and Jesus quotes from the Psalm while on the cross to draw his hearers' attention to the fact that what he was undergoing was in fulfillment of prophecy. Justin makes the same point here.

CHAPTER 36
Different modes of prophecy

But when you hear the utterances of the prophets spoken as it were personally, you must not suppose that they are spoken by the inspired themselves, but by the Divine Word who moves them [1]. For sometimes He declares things that are to come to pass, in the manner of one who foretells the future; sometimes He speaks as from the person of God the Lord and Father of all; sometimes as from the person of Christ; sometimes as from the person of the people answering the Lord or His Father, just as you can see even in your own writers, one man being the writer of the whole, but introducing the persons who converse. And this the Jews who possessed the books of the prophets did not understand, and therefore did not recognize Christ even when He came, but even hate us who say that He has come, and who prove that, as was predicted, He was crucified by them.

Notes

[1] Justin again points to the Divine inspiration of the Scriptures.

Commentary

Justin makes the important point that the prophets spoke from different vantage points at various times. Sometimes they spoke of future events, other times they spoke God's Word to His people, other times they recorded Christ's own words (for example, Psalm 22 as previously mentioned), and sometimes they spoke from the vantage point of the people to whom God was speaking. The point is that in order to properly understand the prophetic writings, the reader has to understand from whose point of view the prophet is speaking. Is it the prophet speaking, God, Christ, or the people? The Jews did not understand this and so failed to see Christ in the Old Testament and therefore did not recognize him when he came.

CHAPTER 37
Utterances of the Father

And that this too may be clear to you, there were spoken from the person of the Father through Isaiah the prophet, the following words: "The ox knoweth his owner, and the ass his master's crib; but Israel doth not know, and My people hath not understood. Woe, sinful nation, a people full of sins, a wicked seed, children that are transgressors, ye have forsaken the Lord [1]." And again elsewhere, when the same prophet speaks in like manner from the person of the Father, "What is the house that ye will build for Me? saith the Lord. The heaven is My throne, and the earth is My footstool [2]." And again, in another place, "Your new moons and your sabbaths My soul hateth; and the great day of the fast and of ceasing from labour I cannot away with; nor, if ye come to be seen of Me, will I hear you: your hands are full of blood; and if ye bring fine flour, incense, it is abomination unto Me: the fat of lambs and the blood of bulls I do not desire. For who hath required this at your hands? But loose every bond of wickedness, tear asunder the tight knots of violent contracts, cover the houseless and naked, deal thy bread to the hungry [3]." What kind of things are taught through the prophets from [the person of] God, you can now perceive.

Notes

[1] cf. Isaiah 1:3

[2] cf. Isaiah 66:1

[3] cf. Isaiah 1:14, 58:6

Commentary

Justin provides some examples pertaining to the various "voices" spoken by the prophets. He here, first, quotes from Isaiah where the prophet spoke the words of God the Father. The theme of these verses is that humanity can not offer anything to God; He is the giver to whom proper worship is owed in response to His good gifts. This is in contrast to the pagan gods to whom the Romans believed they must make sacrifices to appease them and in order to gain some advantage.

CHAPTER 38
Utterances of the Son

And when the Spirit of prophecy speaks from the person of Christ, the utterances are of this sort: "I have spread out My hands to a disobedient and gainsaying people, to those who walk in a way that is not good [1]." And again: "I gave My back to the scourges, and My cheeks to the buffetings; I turned not away My face from the shame of spittings; and the Lord was My helper: therefore was I not confounded: but I set My face as a firm rock; and I knew that I should not be ashamed, for He is near that justifieth Me [2]." And again, when He says, "They cast lots upon My vesture, and pierced My hands and My feet. And I lay down and slept, and rose again, because the Lord sustained Me [3]." And again, when He says, "They spake with their lips, they wagged the head, saying, Let Him deliver Himself [4]." And that all these things happened to Christ at the hands of the Jews, you can ascertain. For when He was crucified, they did shoot out the lip, and wagged their heads, saying, "Let Him who raised the dead save Himself [5]."

Notes

[1] cf. Isaiah 65:2

[2] cf. Isaiah 50:6

[3] cf. Psalm 22:18; Psalm 3:5

[4] cf. Psalm 22:7

[5] cf. Matthew 27:39

Commentary

In the previous chapter, Justin provided examples from the prophets where the Father spoke through them. Similarly, here Justin provides illustrations of where the Son spoke through the prophets. The theme of these examples is the crucifixion of Christ. Justin seeks to point out, therefore, that Christ's crucifixion was foretold in the Old Testament and that Christ spoke through the prophets of his coming suffering.

CHAPTER 39
Direct predictions by the Spirit

And when the Spirit of prophecy speaks as predicting things that are to come to pass, He speaks in this way: "For out of Zion shall go forth the law, and the word of the Lord from Jerusalem. And He shall judge among the nations, and shall rebuke many people; and they shall beat their swords into ploughshares, and their spears into pruning-hooks: nation shall not lift up sword against nation, neither shall they learn war any more [1]."

And that it did so come to pass, we can convince you. For from Jerusalem there went out into the world, men, twelve in number [2], and these illiterate, of no ability in speaking: but by the power of God they proclaimed to every race of men that they were sent by Christ to teach to all the word of God; and we who formerly used to murder one another do not only now refrain from making war upon our enemies, but also, that we may not lie nor deceive our examiners, willingly die confessing Christ. For that saying, "The tongue has sworn, but the mind is unsworn [3]," might be imitated by us in this matter. But if the soldiers enrolled by you, and who have taken the military oath, prefer their allegiance to their own life, and parents, and country, and all kindred, though you can offer them nothing incorruptible, it were verily ridiculous if we, who earnestly long for incorruption, should not endure all things, in order to obtain what we desire from Him who is able to grant it.

Notes

[1] cf. Isaiah 2:3

[2] i.e. the Apostles

[3] Justin references a quote from Euripides' play *Hippolytus*, line 608.

Commentary

Following on the examples provided of the Father and Son speaking through the prophets, Justin here provides an example of the Spirit speaking through the Old Testament prophets. One important point to be observed, then, is that Justin references the three persons of the Holy Trinity. In addition, Justin makes the point that the Word of God has power to convert its hearers, as evidenced by the fact that the Apostles' preaching converted those who heard them to faith and reformed their lives. Finally,

Justin points out that Christians are willing to die for their faith. If soldiers are willing to die for their oaths, how much more are Christians willing to do so, seeing as how they have eternal life as a reward from God.

CHAPTER 40
Christ's Advent foretold

And hear how it was foretold concerning those who published His doctrine and proclaimed His appearance, the above-mentioned prophet and king [1] speaking thus by the Spirit of prophecy "Day unto day uttereth speech, and night unto night showeth knowledge. There is no speech nor language where their voice is not heard. Their voice has gone out into all the earth, and their words to the ends of the world. In the sun hath He set His tabernacle, and he as a bridegroom going out of his chamber shall rejoice as a giant to run his course [2]."

And we have thought it right and relevant to mention some other prophetic utterances of David besides these; from which you may learn how the Spirit of prophecy exhorts men to live, and how He foretold the conspiracy which was formed against Christ by Herod the king of the Jews, and the Jews themselves, and Pilate, who was your governor among them, with his soldiers; and how He should be believed on by men of every race; and how God calls Him His Son, and has declared that He will subdue all His enemies under Him; and how the devils, as much as they can, strive to escape the power of God the Father and Lord of all, and the power of Christ Himself; and how God calls all to repentance before the day of judgment comes.

These things were uttered thus:

"Blessed is the man who hath not walked in the counsel of the ungodly, nor stood in the way of sinners, nor sat in the seat of the scornful: but his delight is in the law of the Lord; and in His law will he meditate day and night. And he shall be like a tree planted by the rivers of waters, which shall give his fruit in his season; and his leaf shall not wither, and whatsoever he doeth shall prosper. The ungodly are not so, but are like the chaff which the wind driveth away from the face of the earth. Therefore the ungodly shall not stand in the judgment, nor sinners in the council of the righteous. For the Lord knoweth the way of the righteous; but the way of the ungodly shall perish [3]."

"Why do the heathen rage, and the people imagine new things? The kings of the earth set themselves, and the rulers take counsel together, against the Lord, and against His Anointed, saying, Let us break their bands asunder, and cast their yoke from us. He that dwelleth in the heavens shall laugh at them, and the Lord shall have them in derision. Then shall He speak to them in His wrath, and vex them in His sore displeasure. Yet have I been set by Him a King on Zion His holy hill, declaring the decree of the Lord.

The Lord said to Me, Thou art My Son; this day have I begotten Thee. Ask of Me, and I shall give Thee the heathen for Thine inheritance, and the uttermost parts of the earth as Thy possession. Thou shall herd them with a rod of iron; as the vessels of a potter shalt Thou dash them in pieces. Be wise now, therefore, O ye kings; be instructed, all ye judges of the earth. Serve the Lord with fear, and rejoice with trembling. Embrace instruction, lest at any time the Lord be angry, and ye perish from the right way, when His wrath has been suddenly kindled. Blessed are all they that put their trust in Him [4]."

Notes

[1] i.e. David

[2] cf. Psalm 19:2

[3] cf. Psalm 1

[4] cf. Psalm 2

Commentary

Justin takes a little excursion here to talk about how the Spirit of God calls all people to repentance and to faith in Him through Christ. Justin quotes all of Psalms 1 and 2 in an effort to bring his readers to this repentance.

CHAPTER 41
The crucifixion predicted

And again, in another prophecy, the Spirit of prophecy, through the same David, intimated that Christ, after He had been crucified, should reign, and spoke as follows: "Sing to the Lord, all the earth, and day by day declare His salvation. For great is the Lord, and greatly to be praised, to be feared above all the gods. For all the gods of the nations are idols of devils; but God made the heavens. Glory and praise are before His face, strength and glorying are in the habitation of His holiness. Give Glory to the Lord, the Father everlasting. Receive grace, and enter His presence, and worship in His holy courts. Let all the earth fear before His face; let it be established, and not shaken. Let them rejoice among the nations. The Lord hath reigned from the tree [1]."

Notes

[1] This is from Psalm 96, although the last verse is not in the Hebrew manuscripts of the Bible: "The Lord hath reigned from the tree." Justin accused the Jews of removing it in his *Dialogue with Trypho* (chapter 73). Other early Church writers also quoted this verse, including Tertullian and Augustine, leading one to believe that it was in some ancient copies of, perhaps, the Septuagint (see, for example, Augustine's *Exposition on Psalm 96*).

Commentary

Justin quotes from Psalm 96 to demonstrate that Christ's crucifixion on the cross was predicted by David in the Old Testament. As mentioned in the note above, however, the key verse used for this argument ("The Lord hath reigned from the tree") is not in the Hebrew copies of the Old Testament. Many Church writers of the first few centuries, though, quoted this verse, so it may have been in earlier copies of the Greek Septuagint. Otherwise, it is hard to explain why Psalm 96 would be used as support for the contention that Christ's crucifixion was foretold; there is nothing else in the Psalm which would lead one to this conclusion except for this missing verse.

CHAPTER 42
Prophecy using the past tense

But when the Spirit of prophecy speaks of things that are about to come to pass as if they had already taken place, — as may be observed even in the passages already cited by me, — that this circumstance may afford no excuse to readers [for misinterpreting them], we will make even this also quite plain. The things which He absolutely knows will take place, He predicts as if already they had taken place. And that the utterances must be thus received, you will perceive, if you give your attention to them. The words cited above, David uttered 1500 years [1] before Christ became a man and was crucified; and no one of those who lived before Him, nor yet of His contemporaries, afforded joy to the Gentiles by being crucified [2]. But our Jesus Christ, being crucified and dead, rose again, and having ascended to heaven, reigned; and by those things which were published in His name among all nations by the apostles, there is joy afforded to those who expect the immortality promised by Him.

Notes

[1] Actually, about 900 years. This is either Justin's mistake or that of a later copyist.

[2] That is to say, Christ is the first - and only - to fulfill the prophecies.

Commentary

Justin makes the point that the prophecies are often spoken in the past tense in the Old Testament because the Spirit knows they will take place. Thus, he speaks as if they had already happened since they will certainly happen.

CHAPTER 43
Responsibility asserted

But lest some suppose, from what has been said by us, that we say that whatever happens, happens by a fatal necessity, because it is foretold as known beforehand, this too we explain [1]. We have learned from the prophets, and we hold it to be true, that punishments, and chastisements, and good rewards, are rendered according to the merit of each man's actions. Since if it be not so, but all things happen by fate, neither is anything at all in our own power. For if it be fated that this man, e.g., be good, and this other evil, neither is the former meritorious nor the latter to be blamed. And again, unless the human race have the power of avoiding evil and choosing good by free choice, they are not accountable for their actions, of whatever kind they be.

But that it is by free choice they both walk uprightly and stumble, we thus demonstrate. We see the same man making a transition to opposite things. Now, if it had been fated that he were to be either good or bad, he could never have been capable of both the opposites, nor of so many transitions. But not even would some be good and others bad, since we thus make fate the cause of evil, and exhibit her as acting in opposition to herself; or that which has been already stated would seem to be true, that neither virtue nor vice is anything, but that things are only reckoned good or evil by opinion; which, as the true word shows, is the greatest impiety and wickedness.

But this we assert is inevitable fate, that they who choose the good have worthy rewards, and they who choose the opposite have their merited awards. For not like other things, as trees and quadrupeds, which cannot act by choice, did God make man: for neither would he be worthy of reward or praise did he not of himself choose the good, but were created for this end; nor, if he were evil, would he be worthy of punishment, not being evil of himself, but being able to be nothing else than what he was made.

Notes

[1] Justin addresses the topic of fatalism here.

Commentary

Justin discusses the charge that everything happens by foreordained fate. He argues that men are free to either choose good or do evil and that therefore they merit the rewards or punishments which come their way. In addition, "good" and "evil" are objective truths, not just subjective opinions. Note, however, that Justin is not specifically referring to salvation here. His emphasis is on the rewards and punishments which come in this life; the point being that everything which happens in this life is not pre-determined and that mankind has freedom in this life to do good or evil.

CHAPTER 44
Not nullified by prophecy

And the holy Spirit of prophecy taught us this, telling us by Moses that God spoke thus to the man first created: "Behold, before thy face are good and evil: choose the good [1]." And again, by the other prophet Isaiah, that the following utterance was made as if from God the Father and Lord of all: "Wash you, make you clean; put away evils from your souls; learn to do well; judge the orphan, and plead for the widow: and come and let us reason together, saith the Lord: And if your sins be as scarlet, I will make them white as wool; and if they be red like as crimson, I will make them white as snow. And if ye be willing and obey Me, ye shall eat the good of the land; but if ye do not obey Me, the sword shall devour you: for the mouth of the Lord hath spoken it [2]." And that expression, "The sword shall devour you," does not mean that the disobedient shall be slain by the sword, but the sword of God is fire, of which they who choose to do wickedly become the fuel. Wherefore He says, "The sword shall devour you: for the mouth of the Lord hath spoken it." And if He had spoken concerning a sword that cuts and at once despatches, He would not have said, shall devour.

And so, too, Plato, when he says, "The blame is his who chooses, and God is blameless," took this from the prophet Moses and uttered it [3]. For Moses is more ancient than all the Greek writers. And whatever both philosophers and poets have said concerning the immortality of the soul, or punishments after death, or contemplation of things heavenly, or doctrines of the like kind, they have received such suggestions from the prophets as have enabled them to understand and interpret these things. And hence there seem to be seeds of truth among all men; but they are charged with not accurately understanding [the truth] when they assert contradictories.

So that what we say about future events being foretold, we do not say it as if they came about by a fatal necessity; but God foreknowing all that shall be done by all men, and it being His decree that the future actions of men shall all be recompensed according to their several value, He foretells by the Spirit of prophecy that He will bestow meet rewards according to the merit of the actions done, always urging the human race to effort and recollection, showing that He cares and provides for men.

But by the agency of the devils death has been decreed against those who read the books of Hystaspes, or of the Sibyl [4], or of the prophets, that through fear they may prevent men who read them from receiving the knowledge of the good, and may retain them in slavery to themselves; which, however, they could not always effect. For not only do we fearlessly read them, but, as you see, bring them for your inspection, knowing that their contents will be pleasing to all. And if we persuade even a few, our gain will be very great; for, as good husbandmen, we shall receive the reward from the Master.

Notes

[1] cf. Deuteronomy 30:15,19

[2] cf. Isaiah 1:16ff

[3] cf. Plato's *Republic*, book 10

[4] i.e Pagan oracles, although Justin seems to intimate that perhaps there is some good in reading these as containing glimmers of the truth.

Commentary

Justin again argues for the preeminence of the Old Testament prophets. His point is that they spoke the Word of God and that the philosophers took their knowledge from the prophets. Yet, the philosophers did not fully understand the prophets, and so they introduced corruptions and contradictions in their own works. Christians, however, bring the prophetic Scriptures before the world so that all may know the truth in full.

CHAPTER 45
Christ's session in heaven foretold

And that God the Father of all would bring Christ to heaven after He had raised Him from the dead, and would keep Him there until He has subdued His enemies the devils, and until the number of those who are foreknown by Him as good and virtuous is complete, on whose account He has still delayed the consummation — hear what was said by the prophet David. These are his words: "The Lord said unto My Lord, Sit Thou at My right hand, until I make Thine enemies Thy footstool. The Lord shall send to Thee the rod of power out of Jerusalem; and rule Thou in the midst of Thine enemies. With Thee is the government in the day of Thy power, in the beauties of Thy saints: from the womb of morning [1] have I begotten Thee [2]."

That which he says, "He shall send to Thee the rod of power out of Jerusalem," is predictive of the mighty word, which His apostles, going forth from Jerusalem, preached everywhere; and though death is decreed against those who teach or at all confess the name of Christ, we everywhere both embrace and teach it. And if you also read these words in a hostile spirit, ye can do no more, as I said before, than kill us; which indeed does no harm to us, but to you and all who unjustly hate us, and do not repent, brings eternal punishment by fire.

Notes

[1] Or, alternatively, "before the morning star."

[2] cf. Psalm 110:1ff

Commentary

Justin quotes from Psalm 110 to show that Christ's victory was foretold. In addition, the work of the apostles was to go forth with the Word of God to proclaim Christ to all people. The Christians of Justin's time continue to proclaim Christ, even though they are threatened with death, because civil authority has no more power over them than to kill them. Yet, the judgment which awaits the unrepentant is eternal fire.

CHAPTER 46
The Word in the world before Christ

But lest some should, without reason, and for the perversion of what we teach, maintain that we say that Christ was born one hundred and fifty years ago under Cyrenius, and subsequently, in the time of Pontius Pilate, taught what we say He taught; and should cry out against us as though all men who were born before Him were irresponsible — let let us anticipate and solve the difficulty.

We have been taught that Christ is the first-born of God, and we have declared above that He is the Word of whom every race of men were partakers; and those who lived reasonably [1] are Christians, even though they have been thought atheists; as, among the Greeks, Socrates and Heraclitus [2], and men like them; and among the barbarians [3], Abraham [4], and Ananias, and Azarias, and Mishael [5], and Elias [6], and many others whose actions and names we now decline to recount, because we know it would be tedious. So that even they who lived before Christ, and lived without reason, were wicked and hostile to Christ, and slew those who lived reasonably.

But who, through the power of the Word, according to the will of God the Father and Lord of all, He was born of a virgin as a man, and was named Jesus, and was crucified, and died, and rose again, and ascended into heaven, an intelligent man will be able to comprehend from what has been already so largely said. And we, since the proof of this subject is less needful now, will pass for the present to the proof of those things which are urgent.

Notes

[1] i.e. "with reason" or "with the Word."

[2] Socrates was a 5th century Greek philosopher, and Heraclitus was a Greek philosopher of the 6th century. Both talked of the power of the Logos to conform people to its will.

[3] i.e. barbarians defined as those who were not Greek or Roman

[4] i.e. Abraham of the Old Testament

[5] Justin refers to the three friends of the prophet Daniel mentioned in the Old Testament book of Daniel. Ananias (or Hananiah), Mishael, and

Azarias (or Azariah) were their Hebrew names, but they are better known by their Chaldean names: Shadrach, Meshach, and Abednego, respectively.

[6] i.e. the prophet Elijah

Commentary

Justin makes the argument that those who lived prior to Christ's incarnation who lived "reasonably" or "with the Word" were Christians. He contends that those who recognized the Logos/Word of God are saved for the sake of this Word who became flesh. Justin mentions the Greek philosophers Socrates and Heraclitus as examples (he would likely add Plato also), as well as a selection of the Old Testament faithful. This would mean that the Greek philosophers who were considered atheists by their peers, because they did not worship the pagan gods but rather worshiped God and His Logos, were Christians, according to Justin. The additional point Justin is making is that these "pre-Christ" Christians were consistently persecuted by those who lived "unreasonably" (that is, without the Word).

CHAPTER 47
Desolation of Judea foretold

That the land of the Jews, then, was to be laid waste, hear what was said by the Spirit of prophecy. And the words were spoken as if from the person of the people wondering at what had happened. They are these: "Zion is a wilderness, Jerusalem a desolation. The house of our sanctuary has become a curse, and the glory which our fathers blessed is burned up with fire, and all its glorious things are laid waste: and Thou refrainest Thyself at these things, and hast held Thy peace, and hast humbled us very sore [1]." And ye are convinced that Jerusalem has been laid waste, as was predicted. And concerning its desolation, and that no one should be permitted to inhabit it, there was the following prophecy by Isaiah: "Their land is desolate, their enemies consume it before them, and none of them shall dwell therein [2]." And that it is guarded by you lest any one dwell in it, and that death is decreed against a Jew apprehended entering it, you know very well [3].

Notes

[1] cf. Isaiah 64:10-12

[2] cf. Isaiah 1:7

[3] After the Jewish Bar Kokhba revolt in 132 to 136 AD, the Romans deported the Jews from Judea, merged the territory with Syria, and renamed Jerusalem "Aelia Capitolina," barring Jews from the land.

Commentary

The point here is that even the destruction of Jerusalem and Judea was foretold in the Old Testament. The Romans would be very familiar with the destruction, since they were the ones who effected it.

CHAPTER 48
Christ's work and death foretold

And that it was predicted that our Christ should heal all diseases and raise the dead, hear what was said. There are these words: "At His coming the lame shall leap as an hart, and the tongue of the stammerer shall be clear speaking: the blind shall see, and the lepers shall be cleansed; and the dead shall rise, and walk about [1]." And that He did those things, you can learn from the Acts of Pontius Pilate [2]. And how it was predicted by the Spirit of prophecy that He and those who hoped in Him should be slain, hear what was said by Isaiah. These are the words: "Behold now the righteous perisheth, and no man layeth it to heart; and just men are taken away, and no man considereth. From the presence of wickedness is the righteous man taken, and his burial shall be in peace: he is taken from our midst [3]."

Notes

[1] cf. Isaiah 35:6

[2] Justin again refers to a collection of reports regularly made by Pontius Pilate to the emperor Tiberius as part of his official duties. This book, if it existed, has been lost to history, although an apocryphal account exists within the fourth century "Gospel of Nicodemus."

[3] cf. Isaiah 57:1

Commentary

Justin again quotes from the Old Testament to demonstrate that Christ's work was foretold, as well as his death and the death of his disciples.

CHAPTER 49
His rejection by the Jews foretold

And again, how it was said by the same Isaiah, that the Gentile nations who were not looking for Him should worship Him, but the Jews who always expected Him should not recognize Him when He came. And the words are spoken as from the person of Christ; and they are these "I was manifest to them that asked not for Me; I was found of them that sought Me not: I said, Behold Me, to a nation that called not on My name. I spread out My hands to a disobedient and gainsaying people, to those who walked in a way that is not good, but follow after their own sins; a people that provoketh Me to anger to My face [1]."

For the Jews having the prophecies, and being always in expectation of the Christ to come, did not recognize Him; and not only so, but even treated Him shamefully. But the Gentiles, who had never heard anything about Christ, until the apostles set out from Jerusalem and preached concerning Him, and gave them the prophecies, were filled with joy and faith, and cast away their idols, and dedicated themselves to the Unbegotten God through Christ.

And that it was foreknown that these infamous things should be uttered against those who confessed Christ, and that those who slandered Him, and said that it was well to preserve the ancient customs, should be miserable, hear what was briefly said by Isaiah; it is this: "Woe unto them that call sweet bitter, and bitter sweet [2]."

Notes

[1] cf. Isaiah 65:1-3

[2] cf. Isaiah 5:20

Commentary

Justin relates how Christ's rejection by the Jews and reception by the Gentiles was foretold. The Gentiles rejoiced at the proclamation of the Savior which was given them by the Apostles.

CHAPTER 50
His humiliation predicted

But that, having become man for our sakes, He endured to suffer and to be dishonored, and that He shall come again with glory, hear the prophecies which relate to this; they are these: "Because they delivered His soul unto death, and He was numbered with the transgressors, He has borne the sin of many, and shall make intercession for the transgressors. For, behold, My Servant shall deal prudently, and shall be exalted, and shall be greatly extolled. As many were astonished at Thee, so marred shall Thy form be before men, and so hidden from them Thy glory; so shall many nations wonder, and the kings shall shut their mouths at Him. For they to whom it was not told concerning Him, and they who have not heard, shall understand. O Lord, who hath believed our report? and to whom is the arm of the Lord revealed? We have declared before Him as a child, as a root in a dry ground. He had no form, nor glory; and we saw Him, and there was no form nor comeliness: but His form was dishonored and marred more than the sons of men. A man under the stroke, and knowing how to bear infirmity, because His face was turned away: He was despised, and of no reputation. It is He who bears our sins, and is afflicted for us; yet we did esteem Him smitten, stricken, and afflicted. But He was wounded for our transgressions, He was bruised for our iniquities, the chastisement of peace was upon Him, by His stripes we are healed. All we, like sheep, have gone astray; every man has wandered in his own way. And He delivered Him for our sins; and He opened not His mouth for all His affliction. He was brought as a sheep to the slaughter, and as a lamb before his shearer is dumb, so He openeth not His mouth. In His humiliation, His judgment was taken away [1]."

Accordingly, after He was crucified, even all His acquaintances forsook Him, having denied Him; and afterwards, when He had risen from the dead and appeared to them, and had taught them to read the prophecies in which all these things were foretold as coming to pass, and when they had seen Him ascending into heaven, and had believed, and had received power sent thence by Him upon them, and went to every race of men, they taught these things, and were called apostles.

Notes

[1] cf. Isaiah 52:13-15; Isaiah 53:1-8

Commentary

Justin quotes a large part of Isaiah 52 and 53 to demonstrate that the Old Testament foretold Christ's suffering and death. Christ himself had to interpret the Old Testament for his disciples in order to open their eyes to see the prophecies in them which pointed to him. After they received the gift of the Holy Spirit on the day of Pentecost, they went out into all the world to proclaim the Gospel of Jesus Christ. Part of this proclamation also entails revealing to people Christ in the Old Testament.

CHAPTER 51
The majesty of Christ

And that the Spirit of prophecy might signify to us that He who suffers these things has an ineffable origin, and rules His enemies, He spake thus: "His generation who shall declare? because His life is cut off from the earth: for their transgressions He comes to death. And I will give the wicked for His burial, and the rich for His death; because He did no violence, neither was any deceit in His mouth. And the Lord is pleased to cleanse Him from the stripe. If He be given for sin, your soul shall see His seed prolonged in days. And the Lord is pleased to deliver His soul from grief, to show Him light, and to form Him with knowledge, to justify the righteous who richly serveth many. And He shall bear our iniquities. Therefore He shall inherit many, and He shall divide the spoil of the strong; because His soul was delivered to death: and He was numbered with the transgressors; and He bare the sins of many, and He was delivered up for their transgressions [1]."

Hear, too, how He was to ascend into heaven according to prophecy. It was thus spoken: "Lift up the gates of heaven; be ye opened, that the King of glory may come in. Who is this King of glory? The Lord, strong and mighty [2]." And how also He should come again out of heaven with glory, hear what was spoken in reference to this by the prophet Jeremiah [3]. His words are: "Behold, as the Son of man He cometh in the clouds of heaven, and His angels with Him [4]."

Notes

[1] cf. Isaiah 53:8-12

[2] cf. Psalm 24:7

[3] Actually from Daniel, not Jeremiah.

[4] cf. Daniel 7:13

Commentary

Justin continues quoting Isaiah 53 to show that Christ's resurrection and glory was foretold. He also quotes from the Psalms and Daniel to similar effect.

CHAPTER 52
Certain fulfillment of prophecy

Since, then, we prove that all things which have already happened had been predicted by the prophets before they came to pass, we must necessarily believe also that those things which are in like manner predicted, but are yet to come to pass, shall certainly happen. For as the things which have already taken place came to pass when foretold, and even though unknown, so shall the things that remain, even though they be unknown and disbelieved, yet come to pass.

For the prophets have proclaimed two advents of His: the one, that which is already past, when He came as a dishonored and suffering Man; but the second, when, according to prophecy, He shall come from heaven with glory, accompanied by His angelic host, when also He shall raise the bodies of all men who have lived, and shall clothe those of the worthy with immortality, and shall send those of the wicked, endued with eternal sensibility, into everlasting fire with the wicked devils.

And that these things also have been foretold as yet to be, we will prove. By Ezekiel the prophet it was said: "Joint shall be joined to joint, and bone to bone, and flesh shall grow again; and every knee shall bow to the Lord, and every tongue shall confess Him [1]." And in what kind of sensation and punishment the wicked are to be, hear from what was said in like manner with reference to this; it is as follows: "Their worm shall not rest, and their fire shall not be quenched [2];" and then shall they repent, when it profits them not. And what the people of the Jews shall say and do, when they see Him coming in glory, has been thus predicted by Zechariah the prophet: "I will command the four winds to gather the scattered children; I will command the north wind to bring them, and the south wind, that it keep not back. And then in Jerusalem there shall be great lamentation, not the lamentation of mouths or of lips, but the lamentation of the heart; and they shall rend not their garments, but their hearts. Tribe by tribe they shall mourn, and then they shall look on Him whom they have pierced; and they shall say, Why, O Lord, hast Thou made us to err from Thy way? The glory which our fathers blessed, has for us been turned into shame [3]."

Notes

[1] cf. Ezekiel 37:7-8; Isaiah 45:24

[2] cf. Isaiah 46:24

[3] cf. Zechariah 12:3-14; Isaiah 43:17; Isaiah 44:11

Commentary

Justin writes of the two Advents of Christ. He also already covered the First Advent in previous chapters. This refers to the incarnation and was characterized by Christ's suffering and death. He appeared to be simply a man and was rejected by men and crucified. Yet, Christ is returning in glory for the resurrection and the judgment; this is his Final Advent. When he returns he will gather his people to himself, but cast out the unrepentant.

CHAPTER 53
Summary of the prophecies

Though we could bring forward many other prophecies, we forbear, judging these sufficient for the persuasion of those who have ears to hear and understand; and considering also that those persons are able to see that we do not make mere assertions without being able to produce proof, like those fables that are told of the so-called sons of Jupiter. For with what reason should we believe of a crucified man that He is the first-born of the unbegotten God, and Himself will pass judgment on the whole human race, unless we had found testimonies concerning Him published before He came and was born as man, and unless we saw that things had happened accordingly — the devastation of the land of the Jews, and men of every race persuaded by His teaching through the apostles, and rejecting their old habits, in which, being deceived, they had their conversation; yea, seeing ourselves too, and knowing that the Christians from among the Gentiles are both more numerous and more true than those from among the Jews and Samaritans?

For all the other human races are called Gentiles [1] by the Spirit of prophecy; but the Jewish and Samaritan races are called the tribe of Israel, and the house of Jacob. And the prophecy in which it was predicted that there should be more believers from the Gentiles than from the Jews and Samaritans, we will produce: it ran thus: "Rejoice, O barren, thou that dost not bear; break forth and shout, thou that dost not travail, because many more are the children of the desolate than of her that hath an husband [2]." For all the Gentiles were "desolate" of the true God, serving the works of their hands; but the Jews and Samaritans, having the word of God delivered to them by the prophets, and always expecting the Christ, did not recognize Him when He came, except some few, of whom the Spirit of prophecy by Isaiah had predicted that they should be saved. He spoke as from their person: "Except the Lord had left us a seed, we should have been as Sodom and Gomorrah [3]." For Sodom and Gomorrah are related by Moses to have been cities of ungodly men, which God burned with fire and brimstone, and overthrew, no one of their inhabitants being saved except a certain stranger, a Chaldean by birth, whose name was Lot; with whom also his daughters were rescued. And those who care may yet see their whole country desolate and burned, and remaining barren.

And to show how those from among the Gentiles were foretold as more true and more believing, we will cite what was said by Isaiah the prophet; for he spoke as follows "Israel is uncircumcised in heart, but the Gentiles are uncircumcised in the flesh [4]." So many things therefore, as these, when they are seen with the eye, are enough to produce conviction and belief in those who embrace the truth, and are not bigoted in their opinions, nor are governed by their passions.

Notes

[1] "Gentile" refers to a nation; thus, the Gentiles are the nations.

[2] cf. Isaiah 54:1

[3] cf. Isaiah 1:9

[4] This is actually from Jeremiah, not Isaiah; cf. Jeremiah 9:26

Commentary

Justin focuses on the fact that the Gentiles are the ones who were overwhelmingly converted by the Spirit. In the Scriptures, there are two groups of people: Israel (the Church) and the Gentiles (the nations). Through Christ, the people of the nations are brought into the Church. Many Jews rejected Christ, however, and so remained outside of the Church. This is the point which Paul also makes in Romans: "For not all who are descended from Israel belong to Israel" (Romans 9:6ff).

CHAPTER 54
Origin of heathen mythology

But those who hand down the myths which the poets have made, adduce no proof to the youths who learn them; and we proceed to demonstrate that they have been uttered by the influence of the wicked demons, to deceive and lead astray the human race. For having heard it proclaimed through the prophets that the Christ was to come, and that the ungodly among men were to be punished by fire, they put forward many to be called sons of Jupiter, under the impression that they would be able to produce in men the idea that the things which were said with regard to Christ were mere marvelous tales, like the things which were said by the poets. And these things were said both among the Greeks and among all nations where they [the demons] heard the prophets foretelling that Christ would specially be believed in; but that in hearing what was said by the prophets they did not accurately understand it, but imitated what was said of our Christ, like men who are in error, we will make plain.

The prophet Moses, then, was, as we have already said, older than all writers; and by him, as we have also said before, it was thus predicted: "There shall not fail a prince from Judah, nor a lawgiver from between his feet, until He come for whom it is reserved; and He shall be the desire of the Gentiles, binding His foal to the vine, washing His robe in the blood of the grape [1]." The devils, accordingly, when they heard these prophetic words, said that Bacchus was the son of Jupiter, and gave out that he was the discoverer of the vine, and they number wine among his mysteries; and they taught that, having been torn in pieces, he ascended into heaven.

And because in the prophecy of Moses it had not been expressly intimated whether He who was to come was the Son of God, and whether He would, riding on the foal, remain on earth or ascend into heaven, and because the name of "foal" could mean either the foal of an ass or the foal of a horse, they, not knowing whether He who was foretold would bring the foal of an ass or of a horse as the sign of His coming, nor whether He was the Son of God, as we said above, or of man, gave out that Bellerophon [2], a man born of man, himself ascended to heaven on his horse Pegasus.

And when they heard it said by the other prophet Isaiah, that He should be born of a virgin, and by His own means ascend into heaven, they pretended that Perseus was spoken of [3]. And when they knew what was said, as has been cited above, in the prophecies written aforetime, "Strong as a giant to run his course [4]," they said that Hercules was strong, and had journeyed over the whole earth [5]. And when, again, they learned that it had been foretold that He should heal every sickness, and raise the dead, they produced Aesculapius [6].

Notes

[1] cf. Genesis 49:10

[2] A hero in Greek mythology.

[3] In Greek mythology, Perseus was believed to be the son of Zeus and Danaë.

[4] cf. Psalm 19:5

[5] Justin probably has in mind the mythical "Twelve Labors of Hercules."

[6] Aesculapius was the Greek god of medicine.

Commentary

Justin presents an interesting argument that the demons tried to create stories which seemed to fulfill the prophecies of the Old Testament. They understood certain aspects of Christ's person and work from the Scriptures and therefore introduced pagan myths which contained aspects of these prophecies. Yet, they did not fully understand the Scriptures, so the myths are imperfect parallels to Christ. The demons did all this in order to cause confusion and to try to make it look like the Christian faith was just another series of myths, like the demons themselves had created.

CHAPTER 55
Symbols of the cross

But in no instance, not even in any of those called sons of Jupiter, did they imitate the being crucified; for it was not understood by them, all the things said of it having been put symbolically. And this, as the prophet foretold, is the greatest symbol of His power and role; as is also proved by the things which fall under our observation. For consider all the things in the world, whether without this form [1] they could be administered or have any community.

For the sea is not traversed except that trophy which is called a sail abide safe in the ship; and the earth is not ploughed without it: diggers and mechanics do not their work, except with tools which have this shape. And the human form differs from that of the irrational animals in nothing else than in its being erect and having the hands extended, and having on the face extending from the forehead what is called the nose, through which there is respiration for the living creature; and this shows no other form than that of the cross. And so it was said by the prophet, "The breath before our face is the Lord Christ [2]." And the power of this form is shown by your own symbols on what are called "vexilla" [banners] and trophies, with which all your state possessions are made, using these as the insignia of your power and government, even though you do so unwittingly [3]. And with this form you consecrate the images of your emperors when they die, and you name them gods by inscriptions.

Since, therefore, we have urged you both by reason and by an evident form, and to the utmost of our ability, we know that now we are blameless even though you disbelieve; for our part is done and finished.

Notes

[1] i.e. the cross

[2] cf. Lamentations 4:20, from the Greek Septuagint translation

[3] The Roman military standards (vexilla, or the singular vexillum) consisted of a cross with a flag draped on it. Later, in the 4th century AD, the emperor Constantine would also place the Chi-Rho symbol above it to denote Christ (the Greek letters Chi and Rho being the first two letters of the name *Christ*).

Commentary

Justin points out that the symbol of the cross is everywhere on the earth. It is pervasive, and the world could not function without it. This demonstrates the importance of Christ and his crucifixion. Justin closes with the statement that he has borne faithful witness to Christian belief and is therefore now blameless before God, even if his readers fail to believe. In this he is perhaps also thinking of Isaiah's commission in Isaiah 6, where Isaiah is told to go proclaim the Word of the Lord to people, even though they will not believe. The prophets task, however, is always to speak the Lord's Word faithfully.

CHAPTER 56
The demons still mislead men

But the evil spirits were not satisfied with saying, before Christ's appearance, that those who were said to be sons of Jupiter were born of him; but after He had appeared, and been born among men, and when they learned how He had been foretold by the prophets, and knew that He should be believed on and looked for by every nation, they again, as was said above, put forward other men, the Samaritans Simon and Menander, who did many mighty works by magic, and deceived many, and still keep them deceived [1].

For even among yourselves, as we said before [2], Simon was in the royal city Rome in the reign of Claudius Caesar, and so greatly astonished the sacred senate and people of the Romans, that he was considered a god, and honored, like the others whom you honor as gods, with a statue. Wherefore we pray that the sacred senate and your people [3] may, along with yourselves, be arbiters of this our memorial, in order that if any one be entangled by that man's doctrines, he may learn the truth, and so be able to escape error; and as for the statue, if you please, destroy it.

Notes

[1] Simon Magus and his successor Menander were 1st century AD Gnostics and magicians who tried to lure people to them and away from the Church.

[2] See chapter 26.

[3] Notice again the formulation: Senate and People of Rome (SPQR).

Commentary

Justin makes the point again that the demons continue to try to mislead people and prevent them from learning the truth. The particular example of Simon Magus and Menander is provided.

CHAPTER 57
And cause persecution

Nor can the devils persuade men that there will be no conflagration for the punishment of the wicked; as they were unable to effect that Christ should be hidden after He came. But this only can they effect, that they who live irrationally, and were brought up licentiously in wicked customs, and are prejudiced in their own opinions, should kill and hate us; whom we not only do not hate, but, as is proved, pity and endeavor to lead to repentance. For we do not fear death, since it is acknowledged we must surely die; and there is nothing new, but all things continue the same in this administration of things [1]; and if satiety overtakes those who enjoy even one year of these things, they ought to give heed to our doctrines, that they may live eternally free both from suffering and from want. But if they believe that there is nothing after death, but declare that those who die pass into insensibility, then they become our benefactors when they set us free from sufferings and necessities of this life, and prove themselves to be wicked, and inhuman, and bigoted. For they kill us with no intention of delivering us, but cut us off that we may be deprived of life and pleasure.

Notes

[1] cf. Ecclesiastes 1:9-10

Commentary

Justin states that it is the demons who drive men to persecute Christians. The demons were unable to hide the truth of Christ, so now they seek to kill off his disciples. Yet, Christians to not fear death, since death is inevitable - it is only a matter of when a person dies, not if. What is more, Christians believe in the resurrection of the body and the life everlasting. Justin's hope is that those who grow tired of killing Christians will eventually come to the truth, repent, and live.

CHAPTER 58
And raise up heretics

And, as we said before, the devils put forward Marcion of Pontus [1], who is even now teaching men to deny that God is the maker of all things in heaven and on earth, and that the Christ predicted by the prophets is His Son, and preaches another god besides the Creator of all, and likewise another son. And this man many have believed, as if he alone knew the truth, and laugh at us, though they have no proof of what they say, but are carried away irrationally as lambs by a wolf, and become the prey of atheistical doctrines, and of devils. For they who are called devils attempt nothing else than to seduce men from God who made them, and from Christ His first-begotten; and those who are unable to raise themselves above the earth they have riveted, and do now rivet, to things earthly, and to the works of their own hands; but those who devote themselves to the contemplation of things divine, they secretly beat back; and if they have not a wise sober-mindedness, and a pure and passionless life, they drive them into godlessness.

Notes

[1] Marcion was a Gnostic of the late 1st and 2nd centuries AD. He rejected the Old Testament and proposed the existence of a greater god than He who is revealed in the Old Testament. Justin wrote a book specifically to counter his teachings called *Against Marcion*; unfortunately, this book is no longer extant.

Commentary

Another method the demons use to attack the Church is to cause heresy. Thus, the demons persecute the Church to try to kill her people as well as raise up heretics to try to tear the Church apart from within. Marcion is specifically referenced as he was somewhat contemporaneous with Justin and drew people away from the true faith.

CHAPTER 59
Plato's obligation to Moses

And that you may learn that it was from our teachers — we mean the account given through the prophets — that Plato borrowed his statement that God, having altered matter which was shapeless, made the world, hear the very words spoken through Moses, who, as above shown, was the first prophet, and of greater antiquity than the Greek writers; and through whom the Spirit of prophecy, signifying how and from what materials God at first formed the world, spake thus: "In the beginning God created the heaven and the earth. And the earth was invisible and unfurnished, and darkness was upon the face of the deep; and the Spirit of God moved over the waters. And God said, Let there be light; and it was so [1]." So that both Plato and they who agree with him, and we ourselves, have learned, and you also can be convinced, that by the word of God the whole world was made out of the substance spoken of before by Moses. And that which the poets call Erebus, we know was spoken of formerly by Moses [2].

Notes

[1] cf. Genesis 1:1ff

[2] cf. Deuteronomy 32:22. Erebus was the Greek concept of darkness and the underworld; Justin equates it with the Hebrew concept of Sheol.

Commentary

Justin again makes the point that Plato, as well as the other philosophers, received inspiration from the Scriptures, particularly Moses. The Greek philosophers did not always understand the truth, but they came very close to it. Justin cites Genesis here as an example to his readers, showing by whom and with what the world was created. He also obliquely refers to the concept of Sheol, which was the Hebrew word for death and the grave and which the Greeks called Erebus. The point is that the Scriptures are the best source for truth, as they are the only writings inspired by God and pre-date all the philosophers.

CHAPTER 60
Plato's doctrine of the cross

And the physiological discussion concerning the Son of God in the Timaeus of Plato [1], where he says, "He placed him crosswise in the universe [2]," he borrowed in like manner from Moses; for in the writings of Moses it is related how at that time, when the Israelites went out of Egypt and were in the wilderness, they fell in with poisonous beasts, both vipers and asps, and every kind of serpent, which slew the people; and that Moses, by the inspiration and influence of God, took brass, and made it into the figure of a cross, and set it in the holy tabernacle, and said to the people, "If ye look to this figure, and believe, ye shall be saved thereby [3]." And when this was done, it is recorded that the serpents died, and it is handed down that the people thus escaped death.

Which things Plato reading, and not accurately understanding, and not apprehending that it was the figure of the cross, but taking it to be a placing crosswise, he said that the power next to the first God was placed crosswise in the universe. And as to his speaking of a third, he did this because he read, as we said above, that which was spoken by Moses, "that the Spirit of God moved over the waters." For he gives the second place to the Logos which is with God, who he said was placed crosswise in the universe; and the third place to the Spirit who was said to be borne upon the water, saying, "And the third around the third." And hear how the Spirit of prophecy signified through Moses that there should be a conflagration. He spoke thus: "Everlasting fire shall descend, and shall devour to the pit beneath [4]." It is not, then, that we hold the same opinions as others, but that all speak in imitation of ours.

Among us these things can be heard and learned from persons who do not even know the forms of the letters, who are uneducated and barbarous in speech, though wise and believing in mind; some, indeed, even maimed and deprived of eyesight; so that you may understand that these things are not the effect of human wisdom, but are uttered by the power of God.

Notes

[1] The *Timaeus* is Plato's book from about 360 BC where he contemplates the origin and nature of the universe.

[2] cf. *Timaeus* section 1.

[3] cf. Numbers 21:8.

[4] cf. Deuteronomy 32:22

Commentary

Justin furthers his argument that Plato modeled his philosophy on the Hebrew Scriptures. Plato, however, did not completely understand God's revelation and so his teaching is convoluted and not as clear as the Scriptures. Justin says that Plato teaches a Triune God who consists of God, the Logos, and the Spirit. Plato's *Timaeus* is a seminal work of Greek philosophy and very interesting.

CHAPTER 61
Christian baptism

I will also relate the manner in which we dedicated ourselves to God when we had been made new through Christ; lest, if we omit this, we seem to be unfair in the explanation we are making. As many as are persuaded and believe that what we teach and say is true, and undertake to be able to live accordingly, are instructed to pray and to entreat God with fasting, for the remission of their sins that are past, we praying and fasting with them. Then they are brought by us where there is water, and are regenerated in the same manner in which we were ourselves regenerated.

For, in the name of God, the Father and Lord of the universe, and of our Savior Jesus Christ, and of the Holy Spirit, they then receive the washing with water [1]. For Christ also said, "Except ye be born again, ye shall not enter into the kingdom of heaven [2]." Now, that it is impossible for those who have once been born to enter into their mothers' wombs, is manifest to all [3].

And how those who have sinned and repent shall escape their sins, is declared by Isaiah the prophet , as I wrote above [4]; he thus speaks: "Wash you, make you clean; put away the evil of your doings from your souls; learn to do well; judge the fatherless, and plead for the widow: and come and let us reason together, saith the Lord. And though your sins be as scarlet, I will make them white like wool; and though they be as crimson, I will make them white as snow. But if ye refuse and rebel, the sword shall devour you: for the mouth of the Lord hath spoken it [5]."

And for this [rite] we have learned from the apostles this reason. Since at our birth we were born without our own knowledge or choice, by our parents coming together, and were brought up in bad habits and wicked training; in order that we may not remain the children of necessity and of ignorance, but may become the children of choice and knowledge, and may obtain in the water the remission of sins formerly committed, there is pronounced over him who chooses to be born again, and has repented of his sins, the name of God the Father and Lord of the universe; he who leads to the laver the person that is to be washed calling him by this name alone. For no one can utter the name of the ineffable God; and if any one dare to say that there is a name, he raves with a hopeless madness [6]. And this washing is called illumination, because they who learn these things are illuminated in their understandings. And in the name of Jesus Christ, who was crucified under Pontius Pilate, and in the name of the Holy Ghost, who through the prophets foretold all things about Jesus, he who is illuminated is washed.

Notes

[1] i.e. Baptism

[2] cf. John 3:5

[3] cf. John 3:4

[4] See chapter 44

[5] cf. Isaiah 1:16-20

[6] The point being that God does not have names like the pagan's fancied He has. Rather, He is simply God.

Commentary

Justin discusses Christian baptism in this chapter. It is the washing with water for the remission of sins. The one who performs the baptism washes the newly baptized in the name of the Father, Son, and Holy Spirit. Justin writes at a time when the vast majority of those who are baptized are adults; thus, he emphasizes the decision of the one to be baptized. A couple hundred years later, though, infants will increasingly be baptized as the Church grows. The emphasis will then shift to God's saving action through Baptism, rather than the decision or choice of the one baptized. It is the same Baptism, however; God washes away sin with His Word through the water for the sake of Christ who died for sinners.

CHAPTER 62
Its imitation by demons

And the devils, indeed, having heard this washing published by the prophet, instigated those who enter their temples, and are about to approach them with libations and burnt-offerings, also to sprinkle themselves; and they cause them also to wash themselves entirely, as they depart [from the sacrifice], before they enter into the shrines in which their images are set.

And the command, too, given by the priests to those who enter and worship in the temples, that they take off their shoes, the devils, learning what happened to the above-mentioned prophet Moses, have given in imitation of these things. For at that juncture, when Moses was ordered to go down into Egypt and lead out the people of the Israelites who were there, and while he was tending the flocks of his maternal uncle in the land of Arabia, our Christ conversed with him under the appearance of fire from a bush, and said, "Put off thy shoes, and draw near and hear [1]." And he, when he had put off his shoes and drawn near, heard that he was to go down into Egypt and lead out the people of the Israelites there; and he received mighty power from Christ, who spoke to him in the appearance of fire, and went down and led out the people, having done great and marvelous things; which, if you desire to know, you will learn them accurately from his writings.

Notes

[1] cf. Exodus 3:5ff

Commentary

Justin maintains that the demons copied the Christian rite of baptism as well as the act of removing shoes before worship. He refers to Moses conversing with Christ through the burning bush, which is detailed in Exodus 3. More of this will be discussed in the next chapter.

CHAPTER 63
How God appeared to Moses

And all the Jews even now teach that the nameless God spake to Moses; whence the Spirit of prophecy, accusing them by Isaiah the prophet mentioned above, said "The ox knoweth his owner, and the ass his master's crib; but Israel doth not know Me, and My people do not understand [1]." And Jesus the Christ, because the Jews knew not what the Father was, and what the Son, in like manner accused them; and Himself said, "No one knoweth the Father, but the Son; nor the Son, but the Father, and they to whom the Son revealeth Him [2]."

Now the Word of God is His Son, as we have before said. And He is called Angel and Apostle; for He declares whatever we ought to know, and is sent forth to declare whatever is revealed [3]; as our Lord Himself says, "He that heareth Me, heareth Him that sent Me [4]." From the writings of Moses also this will be manifest; for thus it is written in them, "And the Angel of God spake to Moses, in a flame of fire out of the bush, and said, I am that I am, the God of Abraham, the God of Isaac, the God of Jacob, the God of thy fathers; go down into Egypt, and bring forth My people [5]." And if you wish to learn what follows, you can do so from the same writings; for it is impossible to relate the whole here.

But so much is written for the sake of proving that Jesus the Christ is the Son of God and His Apostle, being of old the Word, and appearing sometimes in the form of fire, and sometimes in the likeness of angels; but now, by the will of God, having become man for the human race, He endured all the sufferings which the devils instigated the senseless Jews to inflict upon Him; who, though they have it expressly affirmed in the writings of Moses, "And the angel of God spake to Moses in a flame of fire in a bush, and said, I am that I am, the God of Abraham, and the God of Isaac, and the God of Jacob," yet maintain that He who said this was the Father and Creator of the universe. Whence also the Spirit of prophecy rebukes them, and says, "Israel doth not know Me, my people have not understood Me [6]." And again, Jesus, as we have already shown, while He was with them, said, "No one knoweth the Father, but the Son; nor the Son but the Father, and those to whom the Son will reveal Him [7]."

The Jews, accordingly, being throughout of opinion that it was the Father of the universe who spake to Moses, though He who spake to him was indeed the Son of God, who is called both Angel and Apostle, are justly charged, both by the Spirit of prophecy and by Christ Himself, with knowing neither the Father nor the Son. For they who affirm that the Son is the Father, are proved neither to have become acquainted with the Father, nor to know that the Father of the universe has a Son; who also, being the first-begotten Word of God, is even God. And of old He appeared in the shape of fire and in the likeness of an angel to Moses and to the other prophets; but now in the times of your reign [8], having, as we before said, become Man by a virgin, according to the counsel of the Father, for the salvation of those who believe on Him, He endured both to be set at nought and to suffer, that by dying and rising again He might conquer death.

And that which was said out of the bush to Moses, "I am that I am, the God of Abraham, and the God of Isaac, and the God of Jacob, and the God of your fathers [9]," this signified that they, even though dead, are yet in existence, and are men belonging to Christ Himself. For they were the first of all men to busy themselves in the search after God; Abraham being the father of Isaac, and Isaac of Jacob, as Moses wrote.

Notes

[1] cf. Isaiah 1:3

[2] cf. Matthew 11:27

[3] Angel meaning "messenger" and Apostle meaning "one who is sent with the authority of the sender."

[4] cf. Luke 10:16

[5] cf. Exodus 3:6

[6] cf. Isaiah 1:3

[7] cf. Matthew 11:27

[8] i.e. "the times of your empire," meaning during the reign of the Caesars

[9] cf. Exodus 3:6; also see Mark 12:26-27 where Jesus Christ makes the same point with this passage from Exodus.

Commentary

It is important to note that the early Church fathers (i.e. Christian writers and bishops of the first few centuries) maintained that the pre-incarnate

Christ was present throughout the Old Testament as the one who came personally to meet with his people, particularly Abraham, Jacob, and Moses. In addition, the Old Testament term "Angel of the Lord" or "Angel of God" is believed to refer to the pre-incarnate Christ.

Thus, Justin argues this point in this chapter to show that God the Father has always had a Son and that this Son, the Word of God, conversed with his people throughout the Hebrew Scriptures. Now, during the time of the Roman empire this Word became flesh and revealed himself as Jesus the Christ. He died and then rose again from death in order to accomplish the will of the Father for humanity's salvation, for God "is not God of the dead, but of the living" (Mark 12:27). Of the topic of Christ in the Old Testament and the "Angel of the Lord," may the author humbly suggest his work on this subject entitled *The Christian Story ... as seen through the Old Testament.*

CHAPTER 64
Further misrepresentations of the truth

From what has been already said, you can understand how the devils, in imitation of what was said by Moses, asserted that Proserpine was the daughter of Jupiter, and instigated the people to set up an image of her under the name of Kore [Cora, i.e., the maiden or daughter] at the spring-heads [1]. For, as we wrote above [2], Moses said, "In the beginning God made the heaven and the earth. And the earth was without form and unfurnished: and the Spirit of God moved upon the face of the waters." In imitation, therefore, of what is here said of the Spirit of God moving on the waters, they said that Proserpine [or Cora] was the daughter of Jupiter. And in like manner also they craftily feigned that Minerva was the daughter of Jupiter, not by sexual union, but, knowing that God conceived and made the world by the Word, they say that Minerva is the first conception [ennoia]; which we consider to be very absurd, bringing forward the form of the conception in a female shape [3]. And in like manner the actions of those others who are called sons of Jupiter sufficiently condemn them.

Notes

[1] Proserpine was the goddess, or "maiden" of the underworld and of the spring (i.e. when the rains come).

[2] see Chapter 59

[3] Minerva was supposed to have been born as an adult from the head of Jupiter; she was known as Athena by the Romans.

Commentary

Justin again makes the point that the pagan myths were inspired by the demons in order to mimic Scriptural truths about God. For example, the myth about Proserpine, as the goddess of Spring (when it rains), darkly mimics the fact that the Spirit of God hovered over the waters during the initial creation. In addition, the fact that Jesus was born of a virgin and is God's Son is mimicked in the emergence of Minerva from Jupiter's head. The point being that the demons tried to copy Christian truth in the pagan myths so as to lead people astray.

CHAPTER 65
Administration of the Sacraments

But we, after we have thus washed him who has been convinced and has assented to our teaching, bring him to the place where those who are called brethren are assembled, in order that we may offer hearty prayers in common for ourselves and for the baptized [illuminated] person, and for all others in every place, that we may be counted worthy, now that we have learned the truth, by our works also to be found good citizens and keepers of the commandments, so that we may be saved with an everlasting salvation. Having ended the prayers, we salute one another with a kiss [1].

There is then brought to the president of the brethren bread and a cup of wine mixed with water [2]; and he taking them, gives praise and glory to the Father of the universe, through the name of the Son and of the Holy Ghost, and offers thanks at considerable length for our being counted worthy to receive these things at His hands. And when he has concluded the prayers and thanksgivings, all the people present express their assent by saying Amen. This word Amen answers in the Hebrew language *to genoito* [so be it]. And when the president has given thanks, and all the people have expressed their assent, those who are called by us deacons give to each of those present to partake of the bread and wine mixed with water over which the thanksgiving [3] was pronounced, and to those who are absent they carry away a portion.

Notes

[1] i.e. the kiss of peace which the Apostle Paul also mentions in many of his epistles

[2] Justin is describing the celebration of Communion. This is also known as the Lord's Supper or the Eucharist (meaning *thanksgiving*).

[3] i.e. the Eucharist

Commentary

Justin provides an abbreviated description of the Lord's Supper. One important thing to note is that only the baptized were allowed to participate (and be present during the celebration). In addition, those participating took both the bread and the wine. Finally, the deacons took portions to those who were not present so that they could also participate in the Lord's

Supper. The early Church often called this the Eucharist, which means "thanksgiving." Justin will discuss this in more detail in the following chapter.

CHAPTER 66
Of the Eucharist

And this food is called among us Eucharistia [the Eucharist] [1], of which no one is allowed to partake but the man who believes that the things which we teach are true, and who has been washed with the washing that is for the remission of sins, and unto regeneration [2], and who is so living as Christ has enjoined. For not as common bread and common drink do we receive these; but in like manner as Jesus Christ our Savior, having been made flesh by the Word of God, had both flesh and blood for our salvation, so likewise have we been taught that the food which is blessed by the prayer of His word, and from which our blood and flesh by transmutation are nourished, is the flesh and blood of that Jesus who was made flesh. For the apostles, in the memoirs composed by them, which are called Gospels, have thus delivered unto us what was enjoined upon them; that Jesus took bread, and when He had given thanks, said, "This do ye in remembrance of Me, this is My body [3];" and that, after the same manner, having taken the cup and given thanks, He said, "This is My blood;" and gave it to them alone. Which the wicked devils have imitated in the mysteries of Mithras, commanding the same thing to be done. For, that bread and a cup of water are placed with certain incantations in the mystic rites of one who is being initiated, you either know or can learn [4].

Notes

[1] i.e. thanksgiving

[2] i.e. Baptism

[3] cf. Luke 22:19

[4] The cult of Mithras had ritual meals as part of its mysteries.

Commentary

Justin provides more details concerning the Eucharist, or Lord's Supper. It is only given to those who meet three criteria: (1) they are baptized; (2) they believe the things which are taught; and (3) they are living as Christians ought to live. Thus, it would be assumed (and has been, in fact, common Church practice) not to commune those who are unbaptized, or those who do not believe the things which are taught, or those who are living in open sin. In addition, the bread and wine are not normal bread and wine, but are also the very body and blood of Jesus Christ.

CHAPTER 67
Weekly worship of the Christians

And we afterwards continually remind each other of these things. And the wealthy among us help the needy; and we always keep together; and for all things wherewith we are supplied, we bless the Maker of all through His Son Jesus Christ, and through the Holy Ghost. And on the day called Sunday, all who live in cities or in the country gather together to one place, and the memoirs of the apostles [1] or the writings of the prophets [2] are read, as long as time permits; then, when the reader has ceased, the president verbally instructs, and exhorts to the imitation of these good things. Then we all rise together and pray, and, as we before said, when our prayer is ended, bread and wine and water are brought, and the president in like manner offers prayers and thanksgivings, according to his ability, and the people assent, saying Amen; and there is a distribution to each, and a participation of that over which thanks have been given [3], and to those who are absent a portion is sent by the deacons. And they who are well to do, and willing, give what each thinks fit; and what is collected is deposited with the president, who succors the orphans and widows and those who, through sickness or any other cause, are in want, and those who are in bonds and the strangers sojourning among us, and in a word takes care of all who are in need.

But Sunday is the day on which we all hold our common assembly, because it is the first day on which God, having wrought a change in the darkness and matter, made the world; and Jesus Christ our Savior on the same day rose from the dead [4]. For He was crucified on the day before that of Saturn (Saturday); and on the day after that of Saturn, which is the day of the Sun, having appeared to His apostles and disciples, He taught them these things, which we have submitted to you also for your consideration [5].

Notes

[1] i.e. the Gospels and epistles - what became known as the New Testament

[2] i.e. the Hebrew Scriptures which became known as the Old Testament

[3] i.e. the Eucharist or Holy Communion, the word for communion denoting a "co-participation in" something - in this case the bread and wine and body and blood of the Lord.

[4] i.e. Sunday is the first day of the original creation and the first day of the beginning of the new creation

[5] That is, Christ was crucified on Friday (the day before Saturday) and rose on Sunday (the day after Saturday).

Commentary

Justin provides a concise summary of Christian worship and also provides the reason for Sunday being the day of worship. Christians gather together to read from the Scriptures, pray, hear preaching, and celebrate the Eucharist. This occurs on Sunday because it was the first day of creation and the day of Christ's resurrection.

CHAPTER 68
Conclusion

And if these things seem to you to be reasonable and true, honor them; but if they seem nonsensical, despise them as nonsense, and do not decree death against those who have done no wrong, as you would against enemies. For we forewarn you, that you shall not escape the coming judgment of God, if you continue in your injustice; and we ourselves will invite you to do that which is pleasing to God. And though from the letter of the greatest and most illustrious Emperor Adrian [1], your father, we could demand that you order judgment to be given as we have desired, yet we have made this appeal and explanation, not on the ground of Adrian's decision, but because we know that what we ask is just. And we have subjoined the copy of Adrian's epistle, that you may know that we are speaking truly about this. And the following is the copy: —

Epistle of Adrian [2] in behalf of the Christians:

I have received the letter addressed to me by your predecessor Serenius Granianus, a most illustrious man; and this communication I am unwilling to pass over in silence, lest innocent persons be disturbed, and occasion be given to the informers for practicing villainy. Accordingly, if the inhabitants of your province will so far sustain this petition of theirs as to accuse the Christians in some court of law, I do not prohibit them from doing so. But I will not suffer them to make use of mere entreaties and outcries. For it is far more just, if any one desires to make an accusation, that you give judgment upon it. If, therefore, any one makes the accusation, and furnishes proof that the said men do anything contrary to the laws, you shall adjudge punishments in proportion to the offenses. And this, by Hercules, you shall give special heed to, that if any man shall, through mere calumny, bring an accusation against any of these persons, you shall award to him more severe punishments in proportion to his wickedness.

Notes

[1] i.e. the Roman emperor Hadrian

[2] This is a letter from the Roman emperor Hadrian to Gaius Minucius Fundanus, who was governor of the Roman province of Asia from 122 to 123 AD. The letter is believed to be genuine.

Commentary

Justin closes his letter with a plea to either believe the truth or ignore it, but not to punish Christians with death who have committed no crime. For support for this position, Justin attaches an authentic letter from the emperor Hadrian to the Roman governor of Asia instructing the governor not to allow people to accuse Christians for the mere fact of being Christians. Instead, only those who do something against the law are to be punished. This was Justin's request at the beginning of the letter - i.e. to have Christians judged according to their actions and not on account of the name - and now he closes his letter with the words of the former emperor Hadrian himself making the same case.

SECOND APOLOGY OF JUSTIN MARTYR

CHAPTER 1
Introduction

Romans, the things which have recently happened in your city under Urbicus [1], and the things which are likewise being everywhere unreasonably done by the governors, have compelled me to frame this composition for your sakes, who are men of like passions, and brethren, though ye know it not, and though ye be unwilling to acknowledge it on account of your glorying in what you esteem dignities [2]. For everywhere, whoever is corrected by father, or neighbor, or child, or friend, or brother, or husband, or wife, for a fault, for being hard to move, for loving pleasure and being hard to urge to what is right (except those who have been persuaded that the unjust and intemperate shall be punished in eternal fire, but that the virtuous and those who lived like Christ shall dwell with God in a state that is free from suffering, — we mean, those who have become Christians), and the evil demons, who hate us, and who keep such men as these subject to themselves, and serving them in the capacity of judges, incite them, as rulers actuated by evil spirits, to put us to death. But that the cause of all that has taken place under Urbicus may become quite plain to you, I will relate what has been done.

Notes

[1] Likely Quintus Lollius Urbicus who had governed the Roman province of Britain from 139 AD to 142 AD and later held the post of Prefect of Rome starting in 146 AD; he died in 160 AD. He was a Berber from North Africa.

[2] i.e. the Romans gloried in being Romans

Commentary

Justin begins his Second Apology addressed to the Romans in the city. He says that recent events under Urbicus have caused him to write to them to correct them as a brother, hoping that they will repent. He will explain further in the following chapters.

CHAPTER 2
Urbicus condemns the Christians to death

A certain woman lived with an intemperate husband; she herself, too, having formerly been intemperate [1]. But when she came to the knowledge of the teachings of Christ she became sober-minded, and endeavored to persuade her husband likewise to be temperate, citing the teaching of Christ, and assuring him that there shall be punishment in eternal fire inflicted upon those who do not live temperately and conformably to right reason. But he, continuing in the same excesses, alienated his wife from him by his actions. For she, considering it wicked to live any longer as a wife with a husband who sought in every way means of indulging in pleasure contrary to the law of nature, and in violation of what is right, wished to be divorced from him. And when she was over-persuaded by her friends, who advised her still to continue with him, in the idea that some time or other her husband might give hope of amendment, she did violence to her own feeling and remained with him.

But when her husband had gone into Alexandria, and was reported to be conducting himself worse than ever, she — that she might not, by continuing in matrimonial connection with him, and by sharing his table and his bed, become a partaker also in his wickednesses and impieties — gave him what you call a bill of divorce, and was separated from him. But this noble husband of hers [2], — while he ought to have been rejoicing that those actions which formerly she unhesitatingly committed with the servants and hirelings, when she delighted in drunkenness and every vice, she had now given up, and desired that he too should give up the same, — when she had gone from him without his desire, brought an accusation against her, affirming that she was a Christian. And she presented a paper to thee, the Emperor [3], requesting that first she be permitted to arrange her affairs, and afterwards to make her defense against the accusation, when her affairs were set in order. And this you granted.

And her former husband, since he was now no longer able to prosecute her, directed his assaults against a man, Ptolemaeus, whom Urbicus punished, and who had been her teacher in the Christian doctrines. And this he did in the following way. He persuaded a centurion — who had cast Ptolemaeus into prison, and who was friendly to himself — to take Ptolemaeus and interrogate him on this sole point: whether he were a Christian? And Ptolemaeus, being a lover of truth, and not of a deceitful or false disposition, when he confessed himself to be a Christian, was bound by the centurion, and for a long time punished in the prison.

And, at last, when the man [4] came to Urbicus, he was asked this one question only: whether he was a Christian? And again, being conscious of his duty, and the nobility of it through the teaching of Christ, he confessed his discipleship in the divine virtue. For he who denies anything either denies it because he condemns the thing itself, or he shrinks from confession because he is conscious of his own unworthiness or alienation from it, neither of which cases is that of the true Christian.

And when Urbicus ordered him to be led away to punishment, one Lucius, who was also himself a Christian, seeing the unreasonable judgment that had thus been given, said to Urbicus: "What is the ground of this judgment? Why have you punished this man, not as an adulterer, nor fornicator, nor murderer, nor thief, nor robber, nor convicted of any crime at all, but who has only confessed that he is called by the name of Christian? This judgment of yours, O Urbicus, does not become the Emperor Pius, nor the philosopher, the son of Caesar [5], nor the sacred senate." And he said nothing else in answer to Lucius than this: "You also seem to me to be such an one." And when Lucius answered, "Most certainly I am," he again ordered him also to be led away. And he professed his thanks, knowing that he was delivered from such wicked rulers, and was going to the Father and King of the heavens. And still a third having come forward, was condemned to be punished.

Notes

[1] Intemperate as used here refers to excessiveness and possibly unchastity or adultery.

[2] Justin is being sarcastic by calling her husband "noble."

[3] literally, "to thee, autocrat"

[4] i.e. Ptolemaeus

[5] Justin is probably referring to Marcus Aurelius when he says "the philosopher, the son of Caesar."

Commentary

Justin relates the story of a woman who was accused by her former husband of being a Christian. When he was unable to punish her after her apparently successful defense, he struck out at the man, Ptolemaeus, who had converted her to Christianity. The Roman Prefect Urbicus had

Ptolemaeus executed, as well as a man named Lucius and another man who had taken Urbicus to task for his actions.

CHAPTER 3
Justin accuses Crescens of ignorant prejudice against the Christians

I too, therefore, expect to be plotted against and fixed to the stake, by some of those I have named, or perhaps by Crescens [1], that lover of bravado and boasting; for the man is not worthy of the name of philosopher who publicly bears witness against us in matters which he does not understand, saying that the Christians are atheists and impious, and doing so to win favor with the deluded mob, and to please them. For if he assails us without having read the teachings of Christ, he is thoroughly depraved, and far worse than the illiterate, who often refrain from discussing or bearing false witness about matters they do not understand. Or, if he has read them and does not understand the majesty that is in them, or, understanding it, acts thus that he may not be suspected of being such [a Christian], he is far more base and thoroughly depraved, being conquered by illiberal and unreasonable opinion and fear.

For I would have you to know that I proposed to him certain questions on this subject, and interrogated him, and found most convincingly that he, in truth, knows nothing. And to prove that I speak the truth, I am ready, if these disputations have not been reported to you, to conduct them again in your presence. And this would be an act worthy of a prince. But if my questions and his answers have been made known to you, you are already aware that he is acquainted with none of our matters; or, if he is acquainted with them, but, through fear of those who might hear him, does not dare to speak out, like Socrates [2], he proves himself, as I said before, no philosopher, but a vainglorious man [3]; at least he does not regard that Socratic and most admirable saying: "But a man must in no wise be honored before the truth [4]." But it is impossible for a Cynic, who makes indifference his end, to know any good but indifference [5].

Notes

[1] Crescens was a Cynic philosopher of the 2nd century AD who was opposed to Christianity.

[2] The philosopher Socrates spoke out against what he thought was wrong and was ultimately put to death for his witness to the truth.

[3] literally, "philodoxos" - a lover of glory

[4] cf. Plato's *Republic*, book 10.

[5] The Cynics were known for their "indifference" to life.

Commentary

Justin had run-ins with the Cynic philosopher Crescens who opposed Christianity. Justin says that Crescens does not know about Christianity, has never investigated it, or if he has looked into it does not understand it. He expects that Crescens will try to have him also put to death and therefore offers to debate Crescens before the emperor. Other church writers of the time also characterized Crescens as licentious and no philosopher and believed that he did, in fact, cause Justin's martyrdom.

CHAPTER 4
Why the Christians do not kill themselves

But lest some one say to us, "Go then all of you and kill yourselves, and pass even now to God, and do not trouble us," I will tell you why we do not do so, but why, when examined, we fearlessly confess. We have been taught that God did not make the world aimlessly, but for the sake of the human race; and we have before stated that He takes pleasure in those who imitate His properties, and is displeased with those that embrace what is worthless either in word or deed. If, then, we all kill ourselves, we shall become the cause, as far as in us lies, why no one should be born, or instructed in the divine doctrines, or even why the human race should not exist; and we shall, if we so act, be ourselves acting in opposition to the will of God. But when we are examined, we make no denial, because we are not conscious of any evil, but count it impious not to speak the truth in all things, which also we know is pleasing to God, and because we are also now very desirous to deliver you from an unjust prejudice [1].

Notes

[1] That is, the "unjust prejudice" which the pagans have towards Christians.

Commentary

Justin answers the question of why Christians, if they look forward so much to returning to God, do not just kill themselves. He states that Christians are in the world to teach people the truth and to help make the world better. This is an important theological point; the Church is in the world as "salt" and "light" as Christ said in his Sermon on the Mount (Matthew 5:13-16). Salt seasons and preserves, and light removes the darkness. The people of the Church are sent into the world to perform these functions until Christ returns at the resurrection and judgement to complete the restoration of the world to perfection. The Church looks at the Ark of Noah in a similar manner; the world was preserved on the Ark for the sake of the Church (Noah and his family). For this reason, the Church herself is often characterized as an Ark which protects and preserves, and Noah's Ark is prominent in early Christian art.

CHAPTER 5
How the angels transgressed

But if this idea take possession of some one, that if we acknowledge God as our helper, we should not, as we say, be oppressed and persecuted by the wicked; this, too, I will solve. God, when He had made the whole world, and subjected things earthly to man, and arranged the heavenly elements for the increase of fruits and rotation of the seasons, and appointed this divine law — for these things also He evidently made for man — committed the care of men and of all things under heaven to angels whom He appointed over them.

But the angels transgressed this appointment, and were captivated by love of women, and begat children who are those that are called demons [1]; and besides, they afterwards subdued the human race to themselves, partly by magical writings, and partly by fears and the punishments they occasioned, and partly by teaching them to offer sacrifices, and incense, and libations, of which things they stood in need after they were enslaved by lustful passions; and among men they sowed murders, wars, adulteries, intemperate deeds, and all wickedness.

Whence also the poets and mythologists, not knowing that it was the angels and those demons who had been begotten by them that did these things to men, and women, and cities, and nations, which they related, ascribed them to god himself, and to those who were accounted to be his very offspring, and to the offspring of those who were called his brothers, Neptune and Pluto, and to the children again of these their offspring. For whatever name each of the angels had given to himself and his children, by that name they called them.

Notes

[1] Justin is referring to Genesis 6:1-4.

Commentary

Justin makes an interesting argument that the angels who rebelled against God had children with human women and gave birth to the demons. He bases this argument on the verses in Genesis 6:1-4. This text states: "When man began to multiply on the face of the land and daughters were born to them, the sons of God saw that the daughters of man were attractive. And they took as their wives any they chose. Then the LORD said, 'My Spirit shall not abide in man forever, for he is flesh: his days shall be 120 years.' The Nephilim were on the earth in those days, and also afterward, when the sons of God came in to the daughters of man and they bore children to them. These were the mighty men who were of old, the men of renown."

Many people have debated this verse for centuries. The central issue is the identification of the "sons of God" and the "Nephilim." Some have taken it exactly as Justin interprets it here: rebellious angels and human women had children called "Nephilim." In this interpretation, the "sons of God" are the angels and the Nephilim are the offspring of angels and women.

Others, however, interpret these verses to mean that the men of the Church took wives who were outside of the Church and they had children who were outside of the Church. That is, the faithful intermarried with the unfaithful and this caused the decline of the Church. In this interpretation, the "sons of God" are the men of the Church; i.e. the descendants of Seth. The "daughters of men" are the women of the "un-Church; i.e. the descendants of Cain. The Nephilim are simply their self-righteous children. With this interpretation, God destroyed the world through a flood due to the increasing wickedness of humanity since only eight people (Noah and his family) remained in the Church by Noah's day.

This present author adheres to the second interpretation, rather than to Justin's interpretation. Justin's view, however, fits well within his overall argument that the demons were the gods whom the Romans worshiped.

CHAPTER 6
Names of God and of Christ, their meaning and power

But to the Father of all, who is unbegotten, there is no name given. For by whatever name He be called, He has as His elder the person who gives Him the name [1]. But these words, Father, and God, and Creator, and Lord, and Master, are not names, but appellations derived from His good deeds and functions.

And His Son, who alone is properly called Son, the Word, who also was with Him and was begotten before the works, when at first He created and arranged all things by Him, is called Christ, in reference to His being anointed [2] and God's ordering all things through Him; this name itself also containing an unknown significance; as also the appellation "God" is not a name, but an opinion implanted in the nature of men of a thing that can hardly be explained.

But "Jesus," His name as man and Savior [3], has also significance. For He was made man also, as we before said, having been conceived according to the will of God the Father, for the sake of believing men, and for the destruction of the demons. And now you can learn this from what is under your own observation. For numberless demoniacs throughout the whole world, and in your city, many of our Christian men exorcising them in the name of Jesus Christ, who was crucified under Pontius Pilate, have healed and do heal, rendering helpless and driving the possessing devils out of the men, though they could not be cured by all the other exorcists, and those who used incantations and drugs.

Notes

[1] That is, the one who names something has precedence over the thing he has named.

[2] Christ means "anointed."

[3] Jesus means "Yahweh saves" or "Yahweh is salvation."

Commentary

Justin points out that God has no name. The word "God" is a term used by men who can not quite wrap their minds around Him. Yet, God is called various things which describe His works and nature. Jesus Christ, however, has a name (it should be noted that the name Jesus Christ is given by the Father to him; see Matthew 1:21). He is the anointed Savior, the Word through whom God created all things in the beginning and who came in the flesh to redeem and restore all things. His name has power, as evidenced by the ability of Christians to exorcise demons with his name.

CHAPTER 7
The world preserved for the sake of Christians - man's responsibility

Wherefore God delays causing the confusion and destruction of the whole world, by which the wicked angels and demons and men shall cease to exist, because of the seed of the Christians, who know that they are the cause of preservation in nature [1]. Since, if it were not so, it would not have been possible for you to do these things, and to be impelled by evil spirits; but the fire of judgment would descend and utterly dissolve all things, even as formerly the flood left no one but him only with his family who is by us called Noah, and by you Deucalion [2], from whom again such vast numbers have sprung, some of them evil and others good. For so we say that there will be the conflagration, but not as the Stoics, according to their doctrine of all things being changed into one another, which seems most degrading [3].

But neither do we affirm that it is by fate that men do what they do, or suffer what they suffer, but that each man by free choice acts rightly or sins; and that it is by the influence of the wicked demons that earnest men, such as Socrates and the like, suffer persecution and are in bonds, while Sardanapalus [4], Epicurus [5], and the like, seem to be blessed in abundance and glory.

The Stoics, not observing this, maintained that all things take place according to the necessity of fate. But since God in the beginning made the race of angels and men with free-will, they will justly suffer in eternal fire the punishment of whatever sins they have committed. And this is the nature of all that is made, to be capable of vice and virtue. For neither would any of them be praiseworthy unless there were power to turn to both [virtue and vice].

And this also is shown by those men everywhere who have made laws and philosophized according to right reason, by their prescribing to do some things and refrain from others. Even the Stoic philosophers, in their doctrine of morals, steadily honor the same things, so that it is evident that they are not very felicitous in what they say about principles and incorporeal things. For if they say that human actions come to pass by fate, they will maintain either that God is nothing else than the things which are ever turning, and altering, and dissolving into the same things, and will appear to have had a comprehension only of things that are destructible, and to have looked on God Himself as emerging both in part and in whole in every wickedness; or that neither vice nor virtue is anything; which is contrary to every sound idea, reason, and sense.

Notes

[1] That is to say, it is because of Christians that God reserves and delays judgment on the world.

[2] In Greek myth, Deucalion and his wife survived a flood sent by Zeus by floating on a chest.

[3] The Stoics believed that at death, the soul was received into the Universe. Thus, the person ceased to exist.

[4] Sardanapalus was one of the last kings of Assyria, known for his laziness and licentiousness.

[5] Epicurus was known for his pursuit of pleasure.

Commentary

Justin makes the case that God has delayed His judgment on humanity for the sake of Christians. This, then, leads into a discussion of fate and free-will. Justin maintains that people sin or do good according to their own will and not due to fate.

CHAPTER 8
All have been hated in whom the Word has dwelt

And those of the Stoic school--since, so far as their moral teaching went, they were admirable, as were also the poets in some particulars, on account of the seed of reason [the Logos] implanted in every race of men — were, we know, hated and put to death, — Heraclitus for instance [1], and, among those of our own time, Musonius and others [2]. For, as we intimated, the devils have always effected, that all those who anyhow live a reasonable and earnest life, and shun vice, be hated.

And it is nothing wonderful; if the devils are proved to cause those to be much worse hated who live not according to a part only of the word diffused [among men], but by the knowledge and contemplation of the whole Word, which is Christ. And they, having been shut up in eternal fire, shall suffer their just punishment and penalty. For if they are even now overthrown by men through the name of Jesus Christ, this is an intimation of the punishment in eternal fire which is to be inflicted on themselves and those who serve them. For thus did both all the prophets foretell, and our own teacher Jesus teach.

Notes

[1] Heraclitus was a Greek philosopher of the 6th/5th centuries BC.

[2] Gaius Musonius Rufus was a Romain Stoic philosopher of the 1st century AD.

Commentary

Justin makes special mention of the Stoics, since they came near to Christian virtue and because Marcus Aurelius - one of his intended readers - was a Stoic philosopher in his own right. He makes the point that these philosophers have the Word in part ("diffused"), but Christians have the "whole Word, which is Christ." And Christ is overthrowing the demons and will cast them into hell when he returns.

CHAPTER 9
Eternal punishment is not a mere threat

And that no one may say what is said by those who are deemed philosophers, that our assertions that the wicked are punished in eternal fire are big words and bugbears, and that we wish men to live virtuously through fear, and not because such a life is good and pleasant; I will briefly reply to this, that if this be not so, God does not exist; or, if He exists, He cares not for men, and neither virtue nor vice is anything, and, as we said before, lawgivers unjustly punish those who transgress good commandments.

But since these are not unjust, and their Father teaches them by the word to do the same things as Himself, they who agree with them are not unjust. And if one object that the laws of men are diverse, and say that with some, one thing is considered good, another evil, while with others what seemed bad to the former is esteemed good, and what seemed good is esteemed bad, let him listen to what we say to this.

We know that the wicked angels appointed laws conformable to their own wickedness, in which the men who are like them delight; and the right Reason [1], when He came, proved that not all opinions nor all doctrines are good, but that some are evil, while others are good. Wherefore, I will declare the same and similar things to such men as these, and, if need be, they shall be spoken of more at large. But at present I return to the subject.

Notes

[1] i.e. the Logos or Christ

Commentary

Justin's point is that the Law of God is good. God did not make His Law to punish humanity, but rather to provide them with a guide on how to live good lives which are fulfilling, peaceful, and righteous. He is a kind Father who cares for His creatures and wants them to live well.

CHAPTER 10
Christ compared with Socrates

Our doctrines, then, appear to be greater than all human teaching; because Christ, who appeared for our sakes, became the whole rational being, both body, and reason, and soul. For whatever either lawgivers or philosophers uttered well, they elaborated by finding and contemplating some part of the Word. But since they did not know the whole of the Word, which is Christ, they often contradicted themselves. And those who by human birth were more ancient than Christ, when they attempted to consider and prove things by reason, were brought before the tribunals as impious persons and busybodies.

And Socrates, who was more zealous in this direction than all of them, was accused of the very same crimes as ourselves. For they said that he was introducing new divinities, and did not consider those to be gods whom the state recognized. But he cast out from the state both Homer [1] and the rest of the poets, and taught men to reject the wicked demons and those who did the things which the poets related; and he exhorted them to become acquainted with the God who was to them unknown, by means of the investigation of reason, saying, "That it is neither easy to find the Father and Maker of all, nor, having found Him, is it safe to declare Him to all [2]."

But these things our Christ did through His own power. For no one trusted in Socrates so as to die for this doctrine, but in Christ, who was partially known even by Socrates (for He was and is the Word who is in every man, and who foretold the things that were to come to pass both through the prophets and in His own person when He was made of like passions, and taught these things), not only philosophers and scholars believed, but also artisans and people entirely uneducated, despising both glory, and fear, and death; since He is a power of the ineffable Father, not the mere instrument of human reason [3].

Notes

[1] See Plato's *Republic*, book 10.

[2] See Plato's *Timaeus*, section 1.

[3] i.e. Christ is the Logos of the Father and is not under humanity's control.

Commentary

Justin speaks of the persecution, and death, which Socrates received for denying the pagan gods and urging people to worship the true God. Yet, Socrates saw in part and could not see the whole, because Christ had not yet come in the flesh to reveal God fully. Christians now declare this true God to all people as followers of Christ and are willing to die for this witness. The power of the Word of God draws people to Himself and emboldens them to be faithful to Him.

CHAPTER 11
How Christians view death

But neither should we be put to death, nor would wicked men and devils be more powerful than we, were not death a debt due by every man that is born. Wherefore we give thanks when we pay this debt. And we judge it right and opportune to tell here, for the sake of Crescens and those who rave as he does, what is related by Xenophon [1].

Hercules, says Xenophon, coming to a place where three ways met, found Virtue and Vice, who appeared to him in the form of women: Vice, in a luxurious dress, and with a seductive expression rendered blooming by such ornaments, and her eyes of a quickly melting tenderness, said to Hercules that if he would follow her, she would always enable him to pass his life in pleasure and adorned with the most graceful ornaments, such as were then upon her own person; and Virtue, who was of squalid look and dress, said, But if you obey me, you shall adorn yourself not with ornament nor beauty that passes away and perishes, but with everlasting and precious graces.

And we are persuaded that every one who flees those things that seem to be good, and follows hard after what are reckoned difficult and strange, enters into blessedness. For Vice, when by imitation of what is incorruptible (for what is really incorruptible she neither has nor can produce) she has thrown around her own actions, as a disguise, the properties of virtue, and qualities which are really excellent, leads captive earthly-minded men, attaching to Virtue her own evil properties.

But those who understood the excellences which belong to that which is real, are also uncorrupt in virtue. And this every sensible person ought to think both of Christians and of the athletes, and of those who did what the poets relate of the so-called gods, concluding as much from our contempt of death, even when it could be escaped.

Notes

[1] See Xenophon's *Memorabilia*, 2.1.21ff.

Commentary

Justin relates the story told by Xenophon (a 5th/4th century BC soldier and philosopher) about Hercules' choice between a live of Vice and a life of Virtue. Virtue appears to be boring and plain, but she possesses the promise of future bliss after death. Vice, on the other hand, looks lovely and contains many ornaments, but these things are counterfeits of the real thing. For Vice has no future and so she must present everything up front, while Virtue has the true treasure which she promises her followers. Hercules chose Virtue and endured a tough life, but one with great future rewards. Justin's point is that Christians follow Virtue and therefore do not fear hardship or death, because they look forward to inheriting the treasure of Christ and eternal life with him.

CHAPTER 12
Christians proved innocent by their contempt of death

For I myself, too, when I was delighting in the doctrines of Plato, and heard the Christians slandered, and saw them fearless of death, and of all other things which are counted fearful, perceived that it was impossible that they could be living in wickedness and pleasure. For what sensual or intemperate man, or who that counts it good to feast on human flesh [1], could welcome death that he might be deprived of his enjoyments, and would not rather continue always the present life, and attempt to escape the observation of the rulers; and much less would he denounce himself when the consequence would be death?

This also the wicked demons have now caused to be done by evil men. For having put some to death on account of the accusations falsely brought against us, they also dragged to the torture our domestics, either children or weak women, and by dreadful torments forced them to admit those fabulous actions which they themselves openly perpetrate [2]; about which we are the less concerned, because none of these actions are really ours, and we have the unbegotten and ineffable God as witness both of our thoughts and deeds.

For why did we not even publicly profess that these were the things which we esteemed good, and prove that these are the divine philosophy, saying that the mysteries of Saturn are performed when we slay a man, and that when we drink our fill of blood, as it is said we do, we are doing what you do before that idol you honor, and on which you sprinkle the blood not only of irrational animals, but also of men, making a libation of the blood of the slain by the hand of the most illustrious and noble man among you? And imitating Jupiter and the other gods in sodomy and shameless intercourse with woman, might we not bring as our apology the writings of Epicurus and the poets?

But because we persuade men to avoid such instruction, and all who practice them and imitate such examples, as now in this discourse we have striven to persuade you, we are assailed in every kind of way. But we are not concerned, since we know that God is a just observer of all. But would that even now some one would mount a lofty rostrum, and shout with a loud voice; "Be ashamed, be ashamed, ye who charge the guiltless with those deeds which yourselves openly commit, and ascribe things which apply to yourselves and to your gods to those who have not even the slightest sympathy with them. Be ye converted; become wise."

Notes

[1] Justin is referring to the common false accusations of the pagans against Christians.

[2] That is to say, the accusers are guilty of the very vices of which they accuse Christians.

Commentary

Justin points out that it is ludicrous to suppose that Christians are engaged in lives of vice and pleasure when they so willingly go to their deaths. This willingness to die for their faith is what first intrigued Justin before he was converted himself. For, if Christians really did all the things of which they were accused, would not they try to keep living so they can continue in their pleasures? Yet, the very vices which they are accused of, their accusers themselves do, as do their "gods." The Romans ought to repent of their actions and convert to Christ.

CHAPTER 13
How the Word has been in all men

For I myself, when I discovered the wicked disguise which the evil spirits had thrown around the divine doctrines of the Christians, to turn aside others from joining them, laughed both at those who framed these falsehoods, and at the disguise itself, and at popular opinion; and I confess that I both boast and with all my strength strive to be found a Christian; not because the teachings of Plato are different from those of Christ, but because they are not in all respects similar, as neither are those of the others, Stoics, and poets, and historians. For each man spoke well in proportion to the share he had of the spermatic word, seeing what was related to it [1]. But they who contradict themselves on the more important points appear not to have possessed the heavenly wisdom, and the knowledge which cannot be spoken against.

Whatever things were rightly said among all men, are the property of us Christians. For next to God, we worship and love the Word who is from the unbegotten and ineffable God, since also He became man for our sakes, that becoming a partaker of our sufferings, He might also bring us healing. For all the writers were able to see realities darkly through the sowing of the implanted word that was in them. For the seed and imitation imparted according to capacity is one thing, and quite another is the thing itself, of which there is the participation and imitation according to the grace which is from Him.

Notes

[1] See James 1:21.

Commentary

Justin speaks a little about his own conversion to the faith. In so doing, he points out that all the philosophers had bits of the truth, according to how much of the Word which was in him. Yet, none got it completely correct. It is only now that Christ, the Word in the flesh, has come that God is fully revealed. What was looked at darkly by the philosophers is now revealed clearly (cf. 1 Cor. 13:12). The truth is the possession of Christians, no matter by whom it was spoken. Now Christians reveal to the world the full truth, Christ. He is the Word of God who saves and heals us and for whom all the philosophers were grasping.

CHAPTER 14
Justin prays that his appeal be published

And we therefore pray you to publish this little book, appending what you think right, that our opinions may be known to others, and that these persons may have a fair chance of being freed from erroneous notions and ignorance of good, who by their own fault are become subject to punishment; that so these things may be published to men, because it is in the nature of man to know good and evil [1]; and by their condemning us, whom they do not understand, for actions which they say are wicked, and by delighting in the gods who did such things, and even now require similar actions from men, and by inflicting on us death or bonds or some other such punishment, as if we were guilty of these things, they condemn themselves, so that there is no need of other judges.

Notes

[1] cf. Genesis 3:5.

Commentary

Justin asks that his letter be published so that, hopefully, those who read it will repent and believe in Christ.

CHAPTER 15
Conclusion

And I despised the wicked and deceitful doctrine of Simon [1] of my own nation. And if you give this book your authority, we will expose him before all, that, if possible, they may be converted. For this end alone did we compose this treatise. And our doctrines are not shameful, according to a sober judgment, but are indeed more lofty than all human philosophy: and if not so, they are at least unlike the doctrines of the Sotadists, and Philaenidians, and Dancers, and Epicureans [2], and such other teachings of the poets, which all are allowed to acquaint themselves with both as acted and as written.

And henceforth we shall be silent, having done as much as we could, and having added the prayer that all men everywhere may be counted worthy of the truth. And would that you also, in a manner becoming piety and philosophy [3], would for your own sakes judge justly!

Notes

[1] Justin refers again to Simon Magus.

[2] Various hedonistic philosophies.

[3] Justin makes a word play which refers to the emperors Antoninus Pius and Marcus Aurelius, the philosopher.

Commentary

Justin closes his letter which the prayer that all would believe in the truth of Christ. In comparison to the virtue of Christian faith, he mentions the hedonism of various philosophical systems. If these beliefs are allowed to flourish, why is Christianity - a virtuous faith - persecuted? Justin prays that all people would come to the truth, particularly the emperors Antoninus Pius and Marcus Aurelius, so that they may live up to their monikers of "pious" and "philosopher."

REFERENCES

Ante-Nicene Fathers, The. Ed. Rev. Alexander Roberts and James Donaldson. http://www.ccel.org/ccel/schaff/anf03. html

Augustine. *City of God.* Trans. Henry Bettenson. New York: Penguin Classics, 2004.

Eusebius. The History of the Church. New York: Penguin Books, 1989.

Herodotus. *The Histories.* Trans. Aubrey De Selincourt. Ed. John Marincola. New York: Penguin Books, 2003.

Josephus, Flavius. "The Antiquities of the Jews." *Josephus: The Complete Works.* Trans. William Whiston. Nashville, Tennessee: Thomas Nelson Publishers, 1998.

Josephus, Flavius. "The Wars of the Jews." *Josephus: The Complete Works.* Trans. William Whiston. Nashville, Tennessee: Thomas Nelson Publishers, 1998.

Letters of the Younger Pliny, The. Trans. Betty Radice. New York: Penguin Books, 1969.

Plato. *The Republic.* Trans. Desmond Lee. New York: Penguin Books, 2003.

Plato. *Timaeus and Critias.* Trans. Desmond Lee. New York: Penguin Books, 2008.

Pliny the Elder. *Natural History: A Selection.* Trans. John F. Healy. New York: Penguin Books, 1991.

Simms, Aaron. *The Christian Story: ... as seen through the Old Testament.* St. Polycarp Publishing House, 2014.

Tacitus. *The Annals of Imperial Rome.* Trans. Michael Grant. New York: Penguin Books, 1996.

Tacitus. *The Histories.* Trans. W.H. Fyfe. New York: Oxford University Press, 1997.